DevSecOps: Integrating Security into DevOps

James Relington

DEDICATION

To those who seek knowledge, inspiration, and new perspectives—
may this book be a companion on your journey, a spark for curiosity,
and a reminder that every page turned is a step toward discovery.

AKNOWLEDGEMENTS

I would like to express my deepest gratitude to everyone who contributed to the creation of this book. To my colleagues and mentors, your insights and expertise have been invaluable. A special thank you to my family and friends for their unwavering support and encouragement throughout this journey.

Introduction to DevSecOps

DevSecOps represents a natural and necessary evolution in the world of software development and IT operations. As organizations increasingly rely on digital systems and cloud-native architectures, the demand for rapid software delivery has never been higher. This speed, however, must not come at the expense of security. DevSecOps, short for Development, Security, and Operations, is a methodology that embeds security practices and principles directly into the DevOps workflow. It challenges the traditional notion of treating security as a final step in the development cycle and instead promotes a philosophy where security is integrated from the beginning and maintained throughout the lifecycle of software delivery.

The term DevSecOps might seem like just another industry buzzword, but it represents a profound shift in how teams think about building and delivering secure applications. In the past, security was often the responsibility of a separate team, typically involved only in the later stages of development or during the deployment phase. This siloed approach led to numerous challenges, including delays, miscommunication, and critical vulnerabilities that were discovered too late to be efficiently addressed. DevSecOps aims to eliminate these inefficiencies by fostering collaboration between development, security, and operations teams from the outset.

One of the fundamental ideas behind DevSecOps is the concept of shifting security left. This means incorporating security controls, practices, and thinking as early as possible in the development process. Instead of being an afterthought, security becomes a shared responsibility. Developers are empowered with tools and training to write more secure code, operations teams ensure secure infrastructure configurations, and security experts work alongside everyone to guide decisions and automate checks. This integrated approach enables the detection and remediation of vulnerabilities early in the software lifecycle, where fixes are easier and less expensive to implement.

The rise of DevSecOps is also closely tied to the broader adoption of agile methodologies, cloud computing, and continuous integration/continuous delivery (CI/CD) pipelines. These modern practices prioritize speed, automation, and iteration. They break down traditional development cycles into smaller, faster releases. While this accelerates delivery, it also increases the potential attack surface and reduces the time available for manual security checks. DevSecOps responds to this challenge by emphasizing automation in security practices. Tools for static code analysis, dynamic testing, dependency scanning, container security, and infrastructure-as-code validation are integrated into the pipeline to ensure that security happens at the same speed as development.

However, DevSecOps is not merely a set of tools or scripts added to a CI/CD pipeline. It is primarily a cultural transformation. At its core, it demands a mindset shift from everyone involved in software delivery. Developers, traditionally focused on functionality and performance, must now consider security implications in every line of code. Operations teams must think beyond uptime and availability, taking into account secure configurations and threat monitoring. Security professionals must move from gatekeepers to enablers, helping teams work securely without becoming bottlenecks. This requires communication, collaboration, and a willingness to learn across disciplines.

Another critical component of DevSecOps is education and empowerment. Teams must be trained not just in the tools they use but in the principles of secure development. This includes understanding common vulnerabilities such as SQL injection, cross-site scripting, and misconfigured cloud services. It also involves fostering a proactive security culture where team members feel responsible for identifying and addressing potential issues before they become problems. Empowered teams can make informed decisions and respond quickly to emerging threats, reducing the overall risk to the organization.

The implementation of DevSecOps is not without its challenges. It can be difficult to balance speed and security, especially when deadlines are tight and resources limited. Organizations may struggle with legacy systems, resistance to change, or a lack of skilled personnel. Despite these obstacles, the benefits of adopting DevSecOps are significant. By integrating security into every stage of the software development lifecycle, organizations can reduce vulnerabilities, respond faster to incidents, and build more resilient systems.

DevSecOps also aligns closely with regulatory and compliance requirements. Many industries, such as finance, healthcare, and government, face stringent security mandates. By embedding automated security checks and maintaining detailed audit trails, DevSecOps helps organizations meet these requirements more efficiently. This reduces the burden of manual documentation and reactive fixes, freeing up teams to focus on innovation and improvement.

As cyber threats continue to grow in scale and sophistication, the need for secure-by-design software has become critical. DevSecOps offers a path forward, enabling organizations to build secure, reliable, and scalable applications without sacrificing speed. It represents a more holistic and effective approach to security, one that aligns with the realities of modern software delivery. By treating security as a shared responsibility and integrating it into every aspect of development and operations, DevSecOps creates a culture of security and collaboration that benefits the entire organization.

Understanding the importance and principles of DevSecOps is the first step in this journey. Whether you're a developer, a security professional, an operations engineer, or a business leader, embracing the DevSecOps mindset can help you contribute to creating safer, faster, and more dependable systems. As organizations move forward in a digital-first world, DevSecOps is not just an option — it is a necessity for building trust, maintaining resilience, and staying competitive in an ever-changing threat landscape.

The Evolution from DevOps to DevSecOps

The journey from DevOps to DevSecOps represents a critical shift in the way organizations approach the creation, deployment, and maintenance of software. As the pace of development has accelerated and the complexity of applications has increased, the need to embed security within every stage of the software lifecycle has become undeniable. DevOps was originally conceived as a way to bridge the gap between development and operations, breaking down silos and enabling faster, more reliable software delivery. It emphasized automation, continuous integration, continuous delivery, and a culture of shared responsibility. While DevOps brought incredible gains in speed and efficiency, it often left a crucial component behind: security.

In the early days of DevOps, the primary focus was on speed and collaboration. Developers and operations teams began working more closely, using shared tools and processes to streamline the path from code to production. The result was a dramatic improvement in software delivery cycles. Releases that once took months could now be completed in weeks or even days. Continuous integration and deployment pipelines allowed teams to automate testing, configuration, and deployment tasks. These innovations allowed organizations to respond more quickly to market demands and user feedback. However, the increased speed and automation also introduced new risks. As code was pushed into production faster than ever before, there was often little time for thorough security reviews. Vulnerabilities could go unnoticed, and misconfigurations in infrastructure could lead to serious breaches.

Traditional security models were ill-suited for this new landscape. Security teams, operating separately from development and operations, would typically review software only at the end of the development cycle. This created bottlenecks and led to friction between teams. Developers would see security as a barrier to progress, while security teams would struggle to keep up with the rapid pace of change. In many cases, security reviews were rushed or postponed, increasing the likelihood of insecure code being released into production. The growing number of security incidents and data breaches highlighted the shortcomings of this fragmented approach.

The rise of DevSecOps marked an inflection point in this evolution. It became clear that in order to maintain both speed and security, organizations needed to integrate security into the very fabric of the DevOps process. DevSecOps extends the principles of DevOps by embedding security practices and controls throughout the entire software lifecycle. Rather than treating security as an isolated function, DevSecOps promotes the idea of security as a shared responsibility. Developers, operations engineers, and security professionals all work together, leveraging automation and collaboration to build secure systems from the ground up.

This evolution did not happen overnight. It emerged from a growing recognition within the industry that security must evolve in parallel with development and operations. As microservices, containers, and cloud-native architectures became more widespread, the attack surface expanded significantly. Applications were no longer deployed as monolithic packages on a single server. Instead, they were composed of numerous distributed components, often running in dynamic environments such as Kubernetes clusters or serverless platforms. Securing these systems required a new level of agility and coordination. DevSecOps provided the framework and mindset necessary to meet this challenge.

The transition from DevOps to DevSecOps also coincided with a broader cultural shift within organizations. Security professionals began to move away from the role of enforcers and gatekeepers and instead adopted the role of enablers and collaborators. They worked with developers to understand the pressures of rapid delivery and helped integrate security tools and practices into existing workflows. At the same time, developers began to embrace their role in securing the code they wrote. They learned about common vulnerabilities, implemented secure coding practices, and used automated tools to identify issues early. Operations teams, too, started to prioritize security in their configurations, monitoring, and incident response processes.

Automation played a central role in this transformation. By integrating security tools directly into the CI/CD pipeline, teams could detect vulnerabilities and misconfigurations as part of their standard workflow. Static application security testing (SAST), dynamic application security testing (DAST), software composition analysis (SCA), and infrastructure-as-code (IaC) scanning became routine steps in the development process. These tools provided fast, actionable feedback, allowing teams to fix issues before they reached production. The use of security as code and policy as code enabled teams to define and enforce security rules programmatically, further reducing the reliance on manual intervention.

The evolution from DevOps to DevSecOps also reflected a shift in organizational priorities. Security was no longer seen as a cost center or a compliance checkbox. It became an essential element of business success. Customers, partners, and regulators increasingly demanded evidence of secure practices. High-profile breaches served as wake-up calls, demonstrating the financial and reputational damage that could result from weak security. In this context, DevSecOps emerged as a strategic imperative, not just a technical initiative. It aligned security goals with business objectives and empowered teams to build trust through secure, resilient systems.

Importantly, DevSecOps is not the end of the journey. It represents a mindset and a set of practices that continue to evolve. As new technologies and threats emerge, the principles of collaboration, automation, and shared responsibility remain critical. Organizations that successfully adopt DevSecOps are those that recognize security as a continuous process, one that requires constant learning, adaptation, and investment. They foster a culture where security is everyone's job and where innovation and protection go hand in hand.

The path from DevOps to DevSecOps has reshaped the way modern software is built and delivered. It has brought security to the forefront without sacrificing speed or agility. By embedding security into every stage of the development lifecycle and fostering a culture of collaboration and continuous improvement, DevSecOps offers a powerful approach to building safer, faster, and more reliable software in an increasingly complex digital world.

Core Principles of DevSecOps

DevSecOps is more than just a set of tools or a new phase in the evolution of software development. It is a transformative approach rooted in a set of core principles that drive how development, operations, and security teams work together to deliver secure, reliable, and efficient software. These principles form the foundation of the DevSecOps philosophy and help organizations adapt to a world where security must be embedded in every phase of the software development lifecycle. Understanding these principles is essential for any team or organization looking to adopt or mature their DevSecOps practices.

At the heart of DevSecOps is the belief that security must be a shared responsibility across all teams involved in software creation and delivery. Traditionally, security has been treated as a separate domain, with specialized teams responsible for assessing risks and enforcing controls after development work has already been completed. This separation often leads to delays, friction, and missed vulnerabilities. In contrast, DevSecOps integrates security practices directly into the daily work of developers and operations engineers. It encourages everyone to think about security early and often, from writing secure code to configuring infrastructure safely to monitoring systems for suspicious activity. This cultural shift relies heavily on collaboration and communication among roles that have historically operated in isolation.

Another core principle of DevSecOps is automation. As development cycles grow shorter and teams embrace continuous delivery, manual security checks become impractical. To keep up with the speed of modern software delivery, security processes must be automated wherever possible. This includes automating code scans, vulnerability assessments, compliance checks, and even incident detection and response. Automation reduces the risk of human error, increases consistency, and allows teams to identify and fix issues before they reach production. It enables security to scale along with development, ensuring that the growing volume and velocity of software does not come at the cost of increased risk.

Transparency is also a guiding principle in DevSecOps. Teams must have visibility into what is happening at every stage of the software lifecycle. Developers should understand how their code behaves in production and how it may impact security. Operations teams need insight into code changes and potential security implications. Security teams must be able to see how systems are configured and monitored. This visibility is enabled through comprehensive logging, monitoring, and alerting, as well as by sharing information across tools and teams. When teams have access to the same data and understand the context around it, they can make better decisions and respond more quickly to potential threats.

Integration is another vital principle that distinguishes DevSecOps from earlier approaches. Security is not something that can be bolted on at the end of the development process. It must be woven into every stage, from planning and coding to testing and deployment. This means that security tools and processes should be embedded into the same pipelines that teams use for building and releasing software. It also means that security policies and controls should be defined as code and treated with the same rigor and automation as application logic. Integrating security in this way ensures that it is part of the workflow, not a barrier to it.

Resilience is a core goal of DevSecOps and one of its guiding principles. Instead of assuming that systems can be perfectly secured, DevSecOps embraces the reality that incidents and breaches can happen. The focus shifts from prevention alone to detection, response, and recovery. Systems are designed with security in depth, incorporating layers of protection and fail-safes. Teams practice incident response and learn from security events to strengthen their defenses over time. This mindset fosters adaptability and continuous improvement, allowing organizations to remain secure even in a constantly changing threat landscape.

Empowerment is another key principle that underpins successful DevSecOps practices. Teams must be empowered to take ownership of security, with the knowledge, tools, and support necessary to make informed decisions. Developers should be trained in secure coding techniques and given access to security scanning tools that integrate with their development environments. Operations teams should have clear guidelines for configuring systems securely and for responding to incidents effectively. Security professionals must act as enablers, working with other teams to build a culture where security is part of the everyday workflow. Empowerment also means reducing friction and enabling fast feedback, so that security enhancements do not slow down innovation.

The principle of risk-based decision making is also central to DevSecOps. Not all risks are equal, and not all vulnerabilities require the same response. DevSecOps encourages teams to prioritize based on actual impact and likelihood, rather than treating all issues as critical. This approach helps focus limited resources on the most important threats and avoids overwhelming teams with false positives or low-priority tasks. It also supports a more strategic view of security, aligning it with business goals and operational realities. By understanding the context and consequences of different risks, teams can make smarter choices and build more secure systems.

Finally, continuous improvement lies at the core of DevSecOps. Just as agile development promotes iterative progress, DevSecOps emphasizes the ongoing refinement of security practices. Teams regularly review incidents, analyze metrics, and seek ways to improve their tools, processes, and collaboration. Security is not a one-time goal to be achieved but an evolving challenge that requires vigilance and adaptability. This principle encourages organizations to learn from their experiences, adapt to new threats, and constantly evolve their security posture. It also aligns with the broader DevOps ethos of experimentation, feedback, and rapid iteration.

The core principles of DevSecOps provide a framework for building secure, scalable, and high-performing systems in today's fast-paced technology landscape. By fostering a culture of shared responsibility, prioritizing automation and integration, promoting visibility and empowerment, and committing to resilience and continuous improvement, organizations can create an environment where security is both effective and efficient. These principles are not merely theoretical—they are actionable, practical, and essential for any team seeking to protect their software, their data, and their users in a rapidly evolving digital world.

Benefits of a Security-First Approach

Adopting a security-first approach in software development and operations is no longer a luxury or an afterthought—it is a necessity in today's hyper-connected, threat-prone digital environment. The increasing frequency and sophistication of cyberattacks have forced organizations to rethink how they build and maintain their systems. A security-first mindset means that security is not an isolated phase in the development lifecycle but a foundational element that influences every decision from the earliest stages of planning to the final deployment and beyond. This approach brings a wide array of benefits that impact not only the technical quality of software but also the overall health, reputation, and resilience of the organization.

One of the most immediate benefits of a security-first approach is the significant reduction in vulnerabilities and security incidents. When security is treated as a priority from the beginning, developers are more likely to write secure code, use safe libraries, and configure systems with security best practices in mind. Early detection of flaws through integrated tools and testing helps prevent issues from being introduced into production environments. This proactive stance is far more effective than reactive firefighting, where vulnerabilities discovered post-deployment often require costly emergency fixes, downtime, or even public disclosures. By catching issues early, organizations save time, money, and resources that would otherwise be spent on damage control.

Another major advantage is improved product quality and reliability. Security and quality often go hand in hand. Secure applications tend to be more stable because they avoid risky patterns and enforce stricter controls. Practices like input validation, secure error handling, and proper access management lead to systems that behave more predictably under stress and are less likely to crash or behave unexpectedly. A security-first approach encourages rigorous testing, thoughtful design, and clean code—all of which contribute to a better overall user experience. Customers and end-users benefit from applications that are not only functional but also safe to use, enhancing trust in the product.

The security-first mindset also supports faster and more efficient development cycles over time. Although it may seem counterintuitive, building security into the development process does not slow teams down—it actually enables them to move more confidently and quickly. When security controls and checks are automated and integrated into CI/CD pipelines, they become part of the natural flow of work. Developers receive immediate feedback on potential issues, allowing them to correct problems before they become deeply embedded in the codebase. This continuous feedback loop reduces the likelihood of major rework and eliminates the need for last-minute security reviews that delay releases. Teams gain the freedom to innovate, knowing that security is continuously validated throughout their workflow.

Reputation and customer trust are also significantly enhanced through a security-first approach. In a world where news of data breaches spreads rapidly and consumers are increasingly concerned about the safety of their personal information, trust is a critical currency. Organizations that demonstrate a strong commitment to security are more likely to earn and maintain the confidence of their users, partners, and stakeholders. A single breach can cause irreparable damage to a company's brand, leading to customer churn, lost revenue, and legal consequences. On the other hand, transparent security practices, clear communication, and consistent protection of data can set a company apart in competitive markets and become a valuable differentiator.

Regulatory compliance becomes easier and more sustainable when security is embedded into every stage of software development. Industries such as finance, healthcare, government, and e-commerce are subject to strict regulations that mandate specific security controls and audit requirements. Trying to bolt on compliance after development can lead to a rushed, incomplete, and error-prone process. A security-first approach ensures that compliance considerations are addressed proactively. Policies can be defined as code, controls can be automated, and documentation can be generated as a natural output of the development workflow. This not only reduces the effort needed during audits but also ensures that compliance is maintained continuously, rather than checked only at scheduled intervals.

A culture of security awareness and shared responsibility also emerges from this approach. When everyone on the team understands their role in maintaining security, it becomes a natural part of their work rather than a separate burden. Developers are empowered to identify and address issues before they escalate. Operations teams are equipped to detect and respond to threats in real time. Security professionals collaborate as partners rather than enforcers, providing guidance and support instead of simply pointing out flaws. This collaborative atmosphere fosters mutual respect, encourages learning, and results in stronger, more cohesive teams.

From a business perspective, a security-first approach mitigates risk in a way that is measurable and strategic. Cybersecurity threats are no longer limited to technical issues—they are business issues with far-reaching implications. Data loss, intellectual property theft, service disruptions, and reputational damage can have serious financial consequences. By prioritizing security from the start, organizations reduce their exposure to these risks and demonstrate due diligence to customers, investors, and regulators. Risk management becomes more proactive and informed, allowing leaders to make decisions with a clearer understanding of potential consequences.

Innovation is also accelerated in environments where security is treated as an enabler rather than a barrier. When teams are confident in the security of their systems, they can explore new ideas, adopt new technologies, and move quickly without fear of unintended consequences. This agility is especially important in industries where speed to market is critical. Security-first development provides a solid foundation for scaling applications, integrating with external services, and adopting modern architectures such as microservices and serverless computing. It ensures that new features and capabilities are introduced without compromising the integrity of the system.

The benefits of a security-first approach extend across technical, operational, and business dimensions. It results in better software, faster delivery, happier customers, and a more resilient organization. By making security an integral part of every decision and every action, teams are better prepared to face the challenges of an increasingly complex digital world. This mindset not only protects systems and data but also drives excellence, innovation, and trust at every level of the organization.

Understanding the DevSecOps Culture

Understanding the culture of DevSecOps is essential for any organization aiming to implement secure, efficient, and collaborative software development and delivery practices. While many teams focus heavily on tools and automation, the real foundation of DevSecOps lies in its culture. It is a way of thinking, behaving, and collaborating that aligns development, security, and operations toward a common goal: delivering secure, high-quality software at speed. Culture is what determines how people interact with each other, how they handle problems, how they share responsibility, and how they adapt to change. In DevSecOps, culture is not just a supporting element—it is the very core of success.

At its heart, the DevSecOps culture is built on shared responsibility. Traditionally, development teams wrote code, operations teams deployed and maintained infrastructure, and security teams audited systems and raised alerts. These groups often worked in isolation, communicating only when necessary and frequently clashing when priorities conflicted. Developers focused on features and functionality, operations prioritized uptime and stability, and security emphasized risk management and compliance. This separation led to inefficiencies, delays, and friction, especially as software delivery cycles grew shorter and more complex. DevSecOps breaks down these silos and replaces them with a culture of collaboration, where all teams work together from the beginning.

Collaboration in DevSecOps means more than occasional meetings or shared chat channels. It is about deep integration of workflows, responsibilities, and goals. Developers are no longer isolated from security concerns. Instead, they are equipped with knowledge and tools to identify and fix vulnerabilities as they write code. Security professionals no longer function only as gatekeepers at the end of a project. They become active contributors throughout the development process, helping to design secure architectures, define policy as code, and guide threat modeling exercises. Operations teams take an active role in implementing and enforcing security controls in the infrastructure. Everyone is part of the conversation, and everyone contributes to the overall security posture of the organization.

Trust is a central pillar of the DevSecOps culture. For collaboration to be effective, teams must trust each other's expertise, intentions, and commitment. This trust is built through transparency, communication, and a willingness to learn from one another. Developers must trust that security professionals will support rather than block their progress. Security teams must trust that developers are making informed, responsible choices. Operations must trust that both developers and security teams are considering the long-term stability and maintainability of systems. This mutual trust helps eliminate the blame culture that often arises when incidents occur, replacing it with a focus on solutions and continuous improvement.

Psychological safety plays a major role in nurturing the DevSecOps culture. Teams must feel comfortable raising concerns, admitting mistakes, and suggesting changes without fear of punishment or ridicule. When people are afraid to speak up, vulnerabilities go unreported, misconfigurations are ignored, and learning is stifled. A culture that encourages curiosity, accountability, and open dialogue allows teams to identify problems early, address root causes, and evolve their practices over time. It also fosters innovation by creating an environment where experimentation is supported and failure is treated as an opportunity to learn.

Another defining trait of the DevSecOps culture is continuous feedback. In traditional models, feedback loops were long and fragmented. Developers might wait weeks or months to hear about a security issue found in their code, by which time the context had been lost and fixing the issue was costly. In DevSecOps, feedback is fast, frequent, and integrated into the development workflow. Automated tools provide real-time insights into code quality, vulnerabilities, and compliance. Logs, metrics, and monitoring dashboards offer continuous visibility into system behavior. This immediate feedback helps teams correct issues quickly, reinforces good practices, and supports a culture of learning and accountability.

Learning and growth are essential components of DevSecOps culture. Security is a fast-moving field, with new threats, tools, and best practices emerging constantly. For teams to stay effective, they must be committed to ongoing education and improvement. Organizations that foster a DevSecOps culture invest in training, workshops, and shared learning opportunities. They encourage team members to explore new technologies, share knowledge, and participate in the broader security and DevOps communities. Leaders play a key role by modeling continuous learning, recognizing progress, and providing the time and resources needed to build skills.

Ownership is also a hallmark of DevSecOps culture. In traditional settings, developers might write code and throw it over the wall to operations or security, absolving themselves of further responsibility. In DevSecOps, everyone owns their work end to end. Developers own the quality and security of the code they produce. Security teams own their contribution to enabling secure delivery. Operations own the resilience and observability of the systems they manage. This sense of ownership leads to higher accountability, better decision-making, and a greater sense of pride in the outcomes.

A strong DevSecOps culture also recognizes that technology is only part of the equation. Even the most advanced tools will fail if teams are not aligned in their goals, values, and behaviors. Culture shapes how tools are selected, how processes are designed, and how problems are solved. It influences whether security is viewed as an obstacle or an enabler, whether incidents are treated as failures or learning moments, and whether teams work together or in conflict. Building a DevSecOps culture means aligning incentives, removing barriers, and creating a shared vision of what secure, efficient, and responsible software delivery looks like.

The adoption of a DevSecOps culture does not happen overnight. It requires intentional effort, leadership support, and the willingness to challenge existing habits and assumptions. It involves aligning people, processes, and technology around the idea that security is everyone's responsibility and that collaboration, trust, and continuous improvement are the keys to success. When this culture takes root, the benefits are transformative. Teams become more agile, security becomes proactive, and organizations become more resilient in the face of evolving threats. More importantly, the workplace becomes a space where people are empowered to do their best work, contribute meaningfully to shared goals, and build systems that are both innovative and secure.

Building a DevSecOps Mindset

Building a DevSecOps mindset involves much more than adopting a new set of tools or modifying workflows. It is about fundamentally reshaping how individuals and teams think about software development, operations, and security. At its core, this mindset is based on the belief that security is not a final step or a separate task delegated to a specialized team, but an ongoing, shared responsibility that should be present throughout the entire lifecycle of software creation and deployment. It is an evolution in thought that challenges long-standing practices and pushes for a deeper integration of disciplines that were once siloed and disconnected.

Developing this mindset requires a cultural and intellectual shift at both the individual and organizational levels. Many professionals who come from traditional IT, development, or security backgrounds have been trained to work within rigid boundaries. Developers are often encouraged to focus solely on functionality, speed, and innovation. Security professionals, on the other hand, are trained to identify risks, block threats, and reduce exposure, sometimes at the expense of agility or convenience. Operations teams are frequently judged by uptime and system stability, and may view any additional complexity—like security controls—as a risk to that stability. The DevSecOps mindset breaks down these traditional walls and encourages a more holistic, integrated approach where security, development, and operations objectives are aligned.

One of the first steps in cultivating this mindset is recognizing the importance of empathy and understanding among different roles.

Developers need to understand the pressures security professionals face in protecting systems against increasingly sophisticated threats. Security experts must appreciate the speed at which developers are expected to deliver new features, often under intense pressure from business leaders. Operations teams must be aware of the intricate dependencies and risks involved in both new deployments and existing infrastructure. When each group takes the time to understand the challenges faced by the others, it becomes easier to collaborate, communicate, and make decisions that balance security, performance, and innovation.

A DevSecOps mindset also demands that individuals become comfortable with continuous change. Unlike traditional project-based security efforts, DevSecOps is built around the idea of continuous integration, continuous testing, continuous delivery, and continuous monitoring. Security is not a checkbox to be marked at the end of a sprint, nor is it a fixed point in time. It is something that must evolve with each code change, each infrastructure update, and each threat that emerges in the wider world. This demands a mental flexibility and an openness to adapting practices, learning new skills, and embracing automation wherever possible.

Automation plays a key role in reinforcing the DevSecOps mindset. By embedding security checks into development pipelines, teams receive real-time feedback about vulnerabilities, configuration errors, and policy violations. This encourages proactive behavior and builds habits around secure development. Developers begin to anticipate issues and write code with security in mind. Security professionals move away from manual, after-the-fact audits and become more involved in the design and implementation phases. Operations teams leverage automated scanning and monitoring to detect and respond to issues before they escalate. Over time, this automation becomes a natural part of the workflow, reinforcing the mindset that security is always present, always active, and always important.

Another essential element in building this mindset is education. A DevSecOps culture cannot thrive if team members lack the knowledge or skills to contribute to security effectively. Training programs, hands-on workshops, and regular knowledge sharing sessions are necessary to help individuals understand secure coding practices, common vulnerabilities, threat modeling, and how to use the tools that support secure development. But education should go beyond technical instruction. It should also include learning how to collaborate across roles, how to give and receive feedback, and how to make decisions that consider multiple perspectives. The goal is to empower every member of the team to see themselves as a part of the security effort, regardless of their formal role.

Leadership also plays a critical part in fostering the DevSecOps mindset. When leaders prioritize security, support collaborative processes, and celebrate team successes related to security, they set the tone for the rest of the organization. Leaders must be willing to invest in tooling, training, and time to allow teams to build secure systems without compromising innovation. They must also be patient, recognizing that cultural change takes time and that mistakes are part of the learning process. By leading with transparency, encouraging accountability, and demonstrating a personal commitment to security, leaders help instill these values throughout their teams.

The DevSecOps mindset also includes a strong emphasis on ownership and accountability. When everyone on a team understands that they are responsible for security, there is a greater sense of pride and investment in the work being done. Developers no longer hand off code and forget about it. They monitor its behavior in production and respond to issues. Security professionals do not simply flag problems— they help solve them and improve processes to prevent future ones. Operations teams do not just maintain systems—they design environments that support secure deployment and ongoing vigilance. This sense of shared responsibility creates stronger, more capable teams that are equipped to respond to challenges together.

Perhaps one of the most transformative aspects of the DevSecOps mindset is its orientation toward resilience. Instead of striving for perfect security—a goal that is ultimately unachievable in a dynamic threat environment—teams focus on building systems that can detect issues, contain damage, and recover quickly. This mindset acknowledges that breaches, failures, and mistakes are inevitable, and prepares organizations to deal with them in a controlled and effective way. It shifts the conversation from fear and blame to preparedness and response. Teams learn from incidents, improve their processes, and grow stronger over time. This not only reduces the impact of security events but also builds confidence in the organization's ability to handle adversity.

Adopting a DevSecOps mindset is not a one-time effort. It requires persistence, commitment, and a willingness to evolve continuously. It means rethinking long-standing habits, questioning old assumptions, and embracing a new way of working where security is integrated into every decision, every line of code, and every system deployed. It means creating an environment where teams are empowered, educated, and united in a shared mission to build secure, reliable, and high-quality software. When this mindset takes hold, the benefits extend far beyond improved security—they lead to better collaboration, higher productivity, and a stronger, more resilient organization ready to thrive in a rapidly changing digital world.

Shifting Security Left

Shifting security left is one of the most essential and transformative principles in the DevSecOps philosophy. At its core, it refers to the practice of introducing security measures and thinking as early as possible in the software development lifecycle. Rather than treating security as a final checkpoint before deployment or as an isolated phase after development, shifting left brings security into the initial stages of planning, design, coding, and testing. This proactive strategy not only reduces the cost and complexity of fixing vulnerabilities but also fosters a more secure-by-design approach across the entire organization. In the traditional software development process, security was often seen as a separate layer of oversight that came into play only after the code was complete or near completion. This approach created significant bottlenecks and delayed releases when security teams identified critical flaws that required reworking large portions of code. It also meant that vulnerabilities had more time to go unnoticed and possibly be exploited. By the time these issues were addressed, developers had often moved on to new projects, forgotten the context of their earlier work, or lacked the resources to make effective fixes. This reactive posture made security feel like an obstacle rather than a partner in progress.

Shifting security left changes this dynamic by embedding security thinking from the very beginning of the development process. It starts with security requirements being discussed during planning meetings alongside feature and performance goals. It means incorporating threat modeling during design phases so teams can anticipate how an attacker might exploit a feature before it is even built. It encourages developers to consider secure coding practices from the moment they begin writing code, supported by training, guidelines, and automated tools that provide immediate feedback. Security becomes a natural part of daily work rather than an external audit looming at the end.

One of the primary benefits of shifting security left is the dramatic improvement in detection speed. When security testing is built into the development pipeline, issues are found in real time or within minutes of code being written. Static analysis tools scan for insecure code patterns, software composition analysis tools examine third-party libraries for known vulnerabilities, and configuration management checks ensure infrastructure as code is not exposing systems to unnecessary risk. These tools integrate directly into version control systems and continuous integration pipelines, allowing developers to receive feedback as part of their normal workflow. This immediacy allows for faster remediation and helps reinforce secure coding habits over time.

Cost is another critical factor in the case for shifting security left. Numerous studies and real-world examples have shown that the earlier a vulnerability is discovered in the development lifecycle, the cheaper it is to fix. A simple bug caught during the design phase might cost a few minutes of redesign, while the same bug found in production could require days of debugging, patching, regression testing, and emergency deployment. It could also result in reputational damage, compliance violations, and financial loss if exploited. By identifying issues early, teams reduce the overall cost of development, speed up delivery, and avoid the resource-draining process of late-stage corrections.

Shifting security left also supports better team collaboration and ownership. When security is embedded early, it naturally becomes a shared responsibility. Developers become more invested in writing secure code because they are involved in the security process from day one. Security professionals are no longer viewed as blockers but as partners who help define and support secure practices from the start. Operations teams gain confidence in the systems being deployed, knowing that security considerations were addressed throughout the development process. This collaborative environment fosters a healthier culture where security is everyone's concern and where teams work together to solve problems, rather than passing blame or working in silos.

Education and empowerment are key enablers of a successful left shift in security. Developers need to be trained in secure coding practices and have access to clear, actionable guidance when they encounter potential issues. Security tools must provide context and explanations, not just alerts, so that developers understand why something is a risk and how to fix it. The goal is not to turn every developer into a security expert, but to give them enough knowledge and support to make safer decisions as they build. When teams are equipped with the right tools and information, they become more autonomous, confident, and capable of integrating security into their daily work.

Another important aspect of shifting security left is changing how organizations approach testing. Traditional approaches often reserve security testing for the final stages of development or after code has been deployed to staging or production environments. In contrast, a left-shifted approach incorporates automated security tests into unit testing, integration testing, and even during code review. Peer reviews can include checks for secure coding standards, while pipelines can automatically enforce security gates that block deployment if high-severity vulnerabilities are detected. These tests are run consistently, with every code change, reducing the risk of regression and ensuring that new features do not introduce unintended weaknesses.

By shifting security left, organizations also position themselves to respond more effectively to changing regulatory landscapes and compliance requirements. When security controls are baked into development processes, it becomes easier to demonstrate compliance with standards such as GDPR, HIPAA, PCI-DSS, or ISO 27001. Auditors can see evidence of security measures embedded throughout the lifecycle, from secure design decisions to code-level protections and automated policy enforcement. This reduces the burden of manual documentation and the risk of non-compliance due to overlooked requirements or rushed last-minute implementations.

Adopting a shift-left mindset also prepares organizations to better handle modern threats. As cyberattacks grow more sophisticated and targeted, waiting until the final stages of development to think about security is no longer viable. Attackers exploit gaps in third-party components, misconfigured APIs, and insufficient authentication logic—issues that are best prevented at the design and code level. By addressing these risks early, teams close off easy attack vectors and make it significantly harder for malicious actors to succeed. This proactive stance strengthens the entire security posture of the organization and builds resilience into its digital products and services.

Ultimately, shifting security left is about creating a safer, more efficient, and more collaborative approach to building software. It aligns with the agile principles of early feedback, continuous improvement, and cross-functional collaboration. It empowers developers to take responsibility for security while equipping them with the tools and support they need to succeed. It transforms security from a roadblock into a catalyst for quality and innovation. As organizations embrace this shift, they build not only more secure systems but also stronger teams and more reliable, trustworthy products.

Threat Modeling in the Development Lifecycle

Threat modeling is a vital practice within the DevSecOps framework, offering a proactive and structured way to identify and address potential security risks before they become real-world vulnerabilities. It is a mental exercise and planning tool that allows teams to think like an attacker and consider how their systems might be exploited. Unlike reactive security measures that only come into play after software has been written or deployed, threat modeling encourages teams to assess risk early in the development lifecycle. By integrating it into the planning and design phases, organizations can build more resilient software and avoid costly security fixes later on.

At its core, threat modeling is about asking critical questions: what are we building, what can go wrong, how can we prevent that from happening, and how do we respond if it does? These questions are simple in form but powerful in practice. When applied consistently and thoughtfully, they help teams uncover weaknesses that may not be visible through automated tools or code scanning alone. Threat modeling forces a deeper understanding of how a system works, how its components interact, and where potential attack vectors lie. It prompts developers, security professionals, and product owners to think beyond functionality and consider the broader implications of design choices.

Integrating threat modeling into the development lifecycle begins during the requirements and architecture phase. This is when systems are at their most malleable, and changes can be made with minimal cost or disruption. At this stage, teams can use threat modeling to evaluate different architectural decisions, select more secure protocols, design more robust authentication flows, and establish better boundaries between components. Identifying threats at this stage means they can be mitigated through design, often eliminating the need for complex controls or reactive patches later on.

One of the strengths of threat modeling is that it encourages cross-functional collaboration. It is most effective when representatives from different disciplines come together to examine a system from multiple perspectives. Developers understand the logic and flow of the code. Security professionals bring knowledge of common vulnerabilities and attack techniques. Operations teams contribute insight into how systems are deployed and maintained in real environments. Product owners and business stakeholders can speak to the value of data, regulatory considerations, and user behavior. This collective knowledge allows for a more comprehensive analysis of potential risks and a more strategic approach to mitigation.

There are several methodologies for conducting threat modeling, each with its own strengths and focus areas. STRIDE, developed by Microsoft, is one of the most commonly used models. It helps teams categorize threats into six types: spoofing, tampering, repudiation, information disclosure, denial of service, and elevation of privilege. This structured approach provides a checklist to ensure that all major threat categories are considered. Another approach is attack tree modeling, where threats are visualized as a hierarchy of possible attack paths, helping teams understand how a series of smaller vulnerabilities might be chained together to cause significant damage. No matter the methodology, the goal remains the same: to anticipate threats before they occur and build in protections as early as possible.

Threat modeling is not a one-time activity but a continuous process that evolves along with the software. As features are added, code is refactored, and infrastructure changes, new threats can emerge. That's why it is important to revisit threat models at key points throughout the development lifecycle. This might include the start of a new sprint, before a major release, or after the integration of a third-party component. Continuous threat modeling ensures that the security posture of the application remains strong and that new risks are addressed before they become exploitable vulnerabilities.

For teams to adopt threat modeling effectively, they need the right mindset, training, and support. Threat modeling should not be seen as a burdensome exercise reserved for security experts. It should be accessible, repeatable, and integrated into the team's normal workflow. Developers can be trained to recognize common patterns of risk and learn how to facilitate basic threat modeling sessions. Security teams can provide templates, tools, and guidance to help teams get started and mature their practices. As teams become more comfortable with threat modeling, it becomes a natural part of the development rhythm, enhancing both the quality and the security of the software being built.

The use of tooling can also support and accelerate threat modeling activities. While the process itself relies heavily on human judgment and creative thinking, there are tools that help document and visualize threats, track mitigations, and integrate findings into issue tracking systems. These tools can be especially useful for large or distributed teams that need to collaborate asynchronously or maintain detailed records for compliance and audit purposes. However, it is essential that tooling supports the process rather than dictates it. The value of threat modeling lies in the discussion, the critical thinking, and the shared understanding it creates among team members.

By embedding threat modeling into the development lifecycle, organizations build a stronger security foundation from the ground up. They reduce the likelihood of surprise vulnerabilities, improve the resilience of their systems, and foster a culture where security is considered at every step. This proactive mindset allows teams to balance innovation with protection, delivering features quickly without sacrificing the integrity of the application. In an era where cyber threats are constantly evolving and attackers are becoming more creative and persistent, threat modeling offers a powerful defense mechanism. It turns security from a reactive function into a strategic design principle and helps teams anticipate the unknown before it becomes a crisis. As part of the broader DevSecOps philosophy, threat modeling represents a commitment to building software that is not only functional and scalable but also secure by design.

Secure Software Development Lifecycle (SSDLC)

The Secure Software Development Lifecycle, or SSDLC, is a structured approach that integrates security practices into every phase of software development. It represents a shift from treating security as a separate or optional concern to embedding it as a core element of the development process. In an age where software is deeply embedded in every aspect of modern life, ensuring the security of applications and systems from the beginning is not just a technical challenge but a fundamental business requirement. The SSDLC framework promotes the design, development, testing, deployment, and maintenance of software with security as a central pillar, reducing risks and enhancing trust in the final product.

Implementing a Secure Software Development Lifecycle begins long before a single line of code is written. The process starts during the requirements and planning phase, where security goals and constraints must be clearly defined. Understanding what kind of data will be processed, who will use the system, and what compliance obligations exist is essential for making informed decisions throughout the rest of the project. Security requirements should be documented alongside functional and performance requirements, not treated as an afterthought. When security is baked into the project from the beginning, teams can make architectural decisions that are more resistant to threats and easier to defend over time.

Designing software with security in mind is a critical component of the SSDLC. During the design phase, teams evaluate different architectural approaches, considering how components will interact and where potential vulnerabilities might emerge. This is where practices like threat modeling become especially valuable. By thinking like an attacker and identifying possible attack vectors, teams can adjust their designs to include stronger authentication mechanisms, enforce least privilege access, segment data flows, and add layers of defense. Design reviews should include security experts and involve a careful examination of how the system will behave under both normal and malicious conditions.

Once development begins, secure coding practices must be consistently followed. Developers should be trained to understand common vulnerabilities such as cross-site scripting, SQL injection, buffer overflows, and insecure deserialization. They should also be familiar with secure design principles like input validation, output encoding, proper error handling, and secure session management. Secure development is supported by coding standards, checklists, and automated tools that identify issues as code is written. Static analysis tools scan source code for patterns that indicate security flaws, providing immediate feedback and helping to enforce good practices before code is committed. Encouraging peer reviews with a focus on security can further enhance the quality and resilience of the codebase.

Testing is a cornerstone of the SSDLC and must include more than just functional validation. Security testing should be part of both manual and automated test suites. Dynamic application security testing tools simulate attacks on running applications to identify weaknesses such as input validation errors and insecure configurations. Penetration testing can provide deep insights into how the application behaves under real-world attack scenarios. Additionally, dependency scanning tools are essential for detecting vulnerabilities in third-party libraries and components, which are often the source of major security incidents. Continuous testing ensures that as the codebase evolves, security gaps do not reappear or expand.

Deployment in a secure software lifecycle is tightly controlled and monitored. Infrastructure as code should be scanned for misconfigurations before deployment, ensuring that environments are not exposing unnecessary services or ports. Secrets such as API keys and database credentials must never be hardcoded or stored in repositories but managed using secure vaults and proper access controls. Configuration management tools help enforce consistency and compliance across environments, reducing the likelihood of errors that could introduce vulnerabilities. Teams should also implement security gates in their CI/CD pipelines, where builds that fail critical security checks are automatically blocked from deployment until resolved.

After deployment, the SSDLC continues through ongoing monitoring, maintenance, and incident response. No system remains static, and new threats or vulnerabilities can emerge at any time. Therefore, it is crucial to continuously monitor logs, user behavior, and system metrics to detect anomalies that may indicate a breach or misuse. Automated alerting and centralized logging support fast response to incidents and aid in forensic investigations. Patch management processes must be efficient and automated where possible, so that known vulnerabilities can be addressed quickly across development, staging, and production environments. Feedback from real-world usage and security incidents should loop back into earlier stages of the lifecycle to guide future development and hardening efforts.

Documentation and governance play an important role in sustaining a secure software development lifecycle. Teams must track how security requirements are met, document architectural decisions, and maintain an audit trail of changes and reviews. This not only supports internal accountability but is often necessary to demonstrate compliance with industry standards and regulations. Governance frameworks help enforce consistent application of security policies and reduce the likelihood that shortcuts or oversights will compromise the system's integrity. Establishing roles and responsibilities, defining workflows, and implementing access control policies are part of a broader strategy to ensure that security is maintained systematically rather than by chance.

Education and awareness are key enablers of a successful SSDLC. Security is not a static discipline, and attackers continuously evolve their tactics. Development and operations teams must be kept up to date with the latest threats, tools, and defensive techniques. Training should be ongoing, and security champions within teams can act as local experts who help disseminate knowledge and drive improvements. A culture that values and rewards secure practices helps ensure that SSDLC principles are followed not just in process documents but in everyday work.

The Secure Software Development Lifecycle is not a rigid checklist or a one-size-fits-all framework. It must be adapted to the unique needs of the organization, the complexity of the systems involved, and the industry context. However, its principles remain consistent: integrate security from the beginning, embed it into every phase of development, and treat it as a shared responsibility. By doing so, teams can create software that is not only functional and performant but also resilient and trustworthy. The SSDLC is a reflection of maturity, foresight, and commitment to building systems that stand up to scrutiny, withstand attacks, and serve users without exposing them to unnecessary risk.

Integrating Security into Agile Frameworks

Integrating security into agile frameworks is one of the most effective ways to ensure that modern software development remains fast, flexible, and secure. Agile methodologies are built around adaptability, short iterative cycles, continuous feedback, and close collaboration across cross-functional teams. These qualities make agile frameworks ideal for delivering software quickly, but they also present unique challenges for incorporating traditional security practices. In the past, security was often viewed as a separate phase at the end of the development cycle, disconnected from the pace and flow of agile teams. This outdated approach creates bottlenecks, introduces risk, and results in missed opportunities to build security into the fabric of the application. When security is aligned with agile values and processes, it becomes an enabler rather than a barrier, enhancing both speed and safety.

The first step to integrating security into agile frameworks is to recognize that security must be included from the very beginning of each sprint, not appended as a final review or post-release audit. In agile planning sessions, when user stories and features are defined, security considerations should be discussed alongside functionality. This means thinking about how new features might introduce vulnerabilities, affect data privacy, or interact with other parts of the system in ways that could be exploited. Including security experts in backlog refinement and sprint planning helps ensure that potential threats are identified early and that appropriate safeguards are built into the work before it begins.

Security-focused tasks should be treated like any other item in the backlog. They need to be estimated, prioritized, and included in sprint commitments. This may involve implementing secure coding practices, integrating security testing tools, addressing known vulnerabilities, or conducting threat modeling exercises for specific features. When security work is part of the sprint and assigned to developers with the same urgency as other tasks, it avoids becoming a last-minute scramble or a neglected afterthought. This approach also reinforces the message that security is a shared responsibility across the entire team.

User stories themselves can be written with security in mind by including acceptance criteria that address security requirements. For example, a user story for account creation might specify that password inputs are encrypted in transit and at rest, that rate limiting is in place to prevent brute-force attacks, or that role-based access control is implemented for different user types. These security criteria make the expected safeguards explicit, testable, and measurable. They also provide a foundation for automated tests that validate the security of features as they are developed.

Automation plays a critical role in bringing security into agile workflows. Agile teams rely heavily on continuous integration and continuous delivery to ensure rapid and reliable releases. By integrating automated security tools into these pipelines, teams can receive immediate feedback on issues such as code vulnerabilities, outdated dependencies, misconfigurations, and compliance violations. Tools like static application security testing, dynamic analysis, and software composition analysis can be run with every code commit or pull request, flagging problems before they make it into the main branch or production environment. These automated checks reduce the burden on manual reviewers and help maintain velocity without sacrificing quality.

To be effective in agile environments, security teams must also adapt their own ways of working. Traditional security review cycles that take weeks are incompatible with sprint cycles that last days. Security professionals need to work closely with developers, participate in daily stand-ups, and be available to answer questions and provide guidance as issues arise. They should act as coaches and collaborators, helping teams understand risks and implement best practices. This close interaction builds trust and accelerates the adoption of secure behaviors. Security teams may also designate security champions within development squads—team members with a passion or background in security who help disseminate knowledge and ensure that security concerns are addressed in every sprint.

Integrating security into agile frameworks also requires a shift in mindset. Agile values individuals and interactions over processes and tools, which means security practices must be lightweight, flexible, and supportive of collaboration. Security policies should be clear, but not overly rigid. Guidelines should empower developers rather than restrict them. The goal is to build a culture where security is seen as an integral part of delivering value to customers. This involves regular education, celebrating secure behaviors, and continuously improving processes based on feedback and lessons learned.

Retrospectives are an important opportunity to reflect on how well security is being integrated into agile work. Teams should ask whether they encountered security issues during the sprint, how they were handled, and what could be improved. These discussions can surface gaps in knowledge, tooling, or process and lead to actionable improvements. By regularly revisiting the security posture of the team, retrospectives help ensure that security remains a living concern and not a static requirement.

Metrics and visibility are also crucial to support security in agile environments. Teams need insight into their current risk posture, the number and severity of security issues identified during sprints, how long those issues remain unresolved, and how often security tasks are completed on time. Dashboards and reports can make this information accessible and actionable, guiding teams to focus on the most critical issues and celebrate progress. Visibility also helps stakeholders, including executives and compliance officers, understand the effectiveness of security efforts and make informed decisions about resourcing and priorities.

When security is truly embedded into agile frameworks, it transforms the way teams build software. Rather than being something external or adversarial, security becomes a core part of the team's identity and process. Features are designed with security in mind, code is written to high standards, and vulnerabilities are caught and fixed quickly. Teams move faster because they are not bogged down by rework or firefighting. They build trust with users, protect the integrity of their systems, and meet regulatory requirements with less stress. Most importantly, they create a foundation for sustainable innovation, where rapid development and strong security go hand in hand.

Choosing the Right DevSecOps Tools

Choosing the right DevSecOps tools is a strategic decision that has long-term implications for the efficiency, security, and success of software development processes. In a DevSecOps environment, where security is deeply embedded into the continuous integration and continuous delivery pipeline, tools are not merely optional add-ons. They form the backbone of automation, enforcement, and observability. With the ever-growing number of tools available in the market, each offering various features and integrations, making the right selection requires a clear understanding of technical needs, team capabilities, and long-term goals. A well-chosen toolchain can empower teams to move quickly while maintaining strong security practices, while poor choices can lead to tool fatigue, inefficiency, and gaps in protection.

The first and perhaps most fundamental consideration when selecting DevSecOps tools is how well they integrate into the existing development pipeline. DevSecOps emphasizes automation and continuous feedback, which means tools must be capable of operating within the same environment where code is written, built, tested, and deployed. This requires seamless compatibility with CI/CD platforms, version control systems, build tools, and container orchestration systems. Tools that interrupt developer workflows, require significant manual intervention, or produce cryptic results will quickly become ignored or resented. The ideal tools are those that feel native to the team's daily operations, surfacing insights exactly when and where they are needed.

Another key factor in tool selection is the ability to support comprehensive coverage across the entire software development lifecycle. A typical DevSecOps pipeline includes multiple stages where security concerns must be addressed, and each stage may require a different category of tooling. During the coding phase, static application security testing tools help identify insecure coding patterns and vulnerabilities directly in the source code. During build and integration, software composition analysis tools examine dependencies and libraries for known vulnerabilities. During runtime, dynamic application security testing and container scanning tools assess applications in their deployed state for vulnerabilities and misconfigurations. Infrastructure-as-code scanning tools evaluate the security posture of environments defined through code. Selecting tools that provide this type of layered coverage ensures that security is applied consistently from start to finish.

Usability is another important aspect that should never be underestimated. Security tools that are too complex, noisy, or unintuitive will fail to gain traction among development teams. Developers must be able to understand and act on the feedback provided by security tools without needing to become security experts themselves. This means that findings should be prioritized by severity and contextualized with clear remediation guidance. Noise must be minimized to avoid alert fatigue. Tools that flag hundreds of low-impact issues without identifying which ones truly matter create more confusion than clarity. In contrast, tools that surface the most critical risks first and provide actionable suggestions empower developers to fix issues quickly and confidently.

Speed and performance also matter significantly. DevSecOps is about moving fast without sacrificing security. Security tools must not introduce unacceptable delays into the pipeline. If scanning tools take too long to complete or block deployments unnecessarily, teams may start to bypass them or disable them altogether. Modern DevSecOps tools are expected to deliver fast feedback, ideally within seconds or minutes, so that security becomes part of the natural rhythm of development. This is especially true for teams practicing trunk-based development or deploying multiple times a day, where even small delays can accumulate into major slowdowns.

Scalability and flexibility should also be evaluated when choosing DevSecOps tools. As teams grow, codebases evolve, and applications become more complex, tools must be able to scale accordingly. They should support distributed teams, microservices architectures, and cloud-native environments. Flexibility in deployment models is also important. Some organizations may prefer cloud-based tools for their ease of use and maintenance, while others may require on-premises solutions due to regulatory or security concerns. The best tools offer a range of deployment options and the ability to adapt to the organization's specific needs and constraints.

Another consideration is how well the tool aligns with compliance and governance requirements. In many industries, organizations must adhere to strict regulations such as GDPR, HIPAA, PCI-DSS, or ISO standards. DevSecOps tools should be able to generate reports, audit trails, and evidence of compliance activities. They should support policy enforcement and allow teams to define and apply security standards programmatically. This not only helps satisfy external auditors but also ensures that internal security policies are consistently applied across all environments.

The ability of a tool to integrate with other tools and systems is also a crucial factor. DevSecOps thrives in environments where information flows freely between systems. Security tools should be able to send alerts to incident response platforms, integrate with ticketing systems to automatically create and track issues, feed data into dashboards and analytics tools, and trigger automated remediation processes. APIs, webhooks, and plugin ecosystems expand the utility of each tool and ensure that security findings lead to real, measurable actions.

Cost and licensing models cannot be ignored, especially for organizations working with limited budgets. While some tools may offer powerful features, their pricing models might not scale well or might be prohibitive for smaller teams. Open-source tools often provide an attractive alternative and can be incredibly effective, especially when combined with in-house expertise. However, open-source tools may require more effort to configure and maintain. Proprietary tools often come with better support and user experience but need to justify their cost with added value. Teams should evaluate both direct and indirect costs, including setup time, maintenance, training, and support.

Finally, the broader ecosystem and community surrounding a tool can have a major impact on its long-term viability. Tools with active communities, frequent updates, and responsive support channels are more likely to remain relevant and improve over time. Community-driven tools often benefit from shared knowledge, plugins, and integrations contributed by other users. Vendor-backed tools with strong documentation and dedicated support teams can provide peace of mind and faster resolution of issues. The strength of a tool's ecosystem often determines how effectively it can be adopted and sustained within an organization.

Choosing the right DevSecOps tools is not just a technical decision; it is a strategic investment in the culture, speed, and security of software development. The best tools are those that integrate smoothly, provide valuable insights, support agile workflows, and empower teams to build secure systems without compromise. When chosen carefully, these tools become enablers of innovation and protectors of trust, helping organizations navigate the complexities of modern development while maintaining strong security and compliance practices.

Code Scanning and Static Analysis

Code scanning and static analysis are fundamental practices in the DevSecOps methodology, playing a crucial role in identifying security flaws and code quality issues early in the software development lifecycle. These techniques provide a proactive way to detect vulnerabilities, logic errors, and non-compliance with coding standards before the application is ever run. By integrating static analysis tools directly into the development workflow, organizations can shift security left and empower developers to address issues during the coding phase, when fixes are faster, easier, and significantly less expensive. This early detection reduces technical debt, enhances software quality, and contributes to a culture of shared responsibility for secure development.

Static analysis involves the automated examination of source code, bytecode, or binary files without executing the program. Unlike dynamic testing, which observes the behavior of a running application, static analysis inspects code structure, syntax, and semantics to uncover vulnerabilities such as buffer overflows, SQL injection, cross-site scripting, hardcoded secrets, and improper error handling. These tools analyze control flow, data flow, and function calls to identify potential flaws in how data is processed, stored, or exposed. The goal is to find weaknesses that could be exploited by an attacker or lead to system instability under certain conditions.

Code scanning tools are often integrated into the developer's integrated development environment or development pipeline, providing immediate feedback as code is written or committed. This continuous analysis model enables real-time detection and remediation of security issues, reducing the risk of vulnerabilities propagating through the lifecycle and making their way into production environments. Developers no longer need to wait for periodic manual reviews or late-stage penetration tests to identify problems. Instead, they are supported with automated checks that guide them toward safer coding patterns and industry best practices.

One of the strengths of static analysis lies in its ability to enforce coding standards and consistency across large codebases and distributed teams. Organizations often establish secure coding guidelines to prevent common vulnerabilities and promote maintainability. Static analysis tools can be configured to enforce these rules, flagging deviations and encouraging adherence to established conventions. This consistency not only improves security but also enhances readability, simplifies code reviews, and reduces onboarding time for new developers. Over time, as teams become more familiar with recurring issues and learn to avoid them proactively, the overall quality and security of the codebase improve significantly.

Despite its advantages, static analysis also has limitations that must be understood and managed. One of the common criticisms is the generation of false positives—warnings about issues that are not truly exploitable or relevant in the given context. Excessive false positives can lead to alert fatigue, causing developers to ignore or dismiss important warnings. To mitigate this, tools must be carefully tuned to balance sensitivity with precision, filtering out noise and focusing attention on high-severity, actionable findings. Context-aware analysis, rule customization, and integration with issue tracking systems help teams prioritize and manage findings more effectively.

Another challenge is the initial learning curve and effort required to integrate static analysis into existing workflows. Teams must evaluate different tools, configure rulesets, and train developers on interpreting and responding to findings. However, this investment pays off over time, as automated scanning becomes a routine part of development and security becomes embedded in the team's mindset. To maximize adoption, it is important to select tools that are easy to use, well-documented, and compatible with the programming languages and frameworks used in the project. User-friendly interfaces, developer-centric reporting, and integration with version control platforms like Git can significantly enhance usability and encourage regular use.

Many static analysis tools support integrations with CI/CD pipelines, making it possible to run scans automatically with every pull request, merge, or build. This tight integration supports a culture of continuous security and helps ensure that new code does not introduce new risks. By enforcing security gates within the pipeline, teams can prevent the deployment of code that fails to meet predefined security criteria. This not only protects production environments but also instills a sense of accountability and ownership among developers, who learn to view security as a natural part of quality control rather than an external constraint.

Open-source and commercial static analysis tools offer a wide range of capabilities, from basic syntax checking to advanced data flow analysis and vulnerability detection. Some tools specialize in specific languages or frameworks, while others provide broad support for multi-language environments. The best tools offer detailed explanations, code samples, and remediation suggestions for each finding, helping developers understand the root cause and learn how to prevent similar issues in the future. This educational component transforms security scans from a compliance task into an opportunity for growth and continuous improvement.

Organizations that adopt static analysis as part of their DevSecOps strategy benefit from earlier discovery of security flaws, improved developer efficiency, and stronger alignment between development and security teams. Static analysis supports compliance efforts by providing evidence of secure coding practices and automated documentation of scans and remediations. It also reduces the burden on manual code reviewers, allowing them to focus on higher-level concerns such as architecture and business logic. When used consistently and intelligently, static analysis becomes a powerful force multiplier, enabling teams to scale security without sacrificing speed or innovation.

In large and fast-moving development environments, where code changes are frequent and deployment cycles are short, the ability to identify and fix security issues before code reaches production is invaluable. Code scanning and static analysis are not silver bullets, but they form a critical part of a layered security approach. When combined with other practices such as dynamic testing, dependency scanning, secure coding standards, and continuous monitoring, they provide a strong foundation for secure and resilient software development. Embracing these tools and integrating them deeply into the daily workflow sends a clear message that security is not optional, but an essential part of delivering high-quality software.

Dynamic Application Security Testing (DAST)

Dynamic Application Security Testing, or DAST, is a crucial technique used to identify vulnerabilities in applications while they are running. Unlike static analysis, which examines source code or binaries without executing them, DAST evaluates an application in its operational state, simulating real-world attack scenarios to uncover weaknesses that might only surface during runtime. This form of black-box testing does not require access to source code, making it especially valuable for assessing third-party applications, legacy systems, or cloud-based services where internal implementation details are unavailable. DAST plays an essential role in a comprehensive DevSecOps strategy, as it provides visibility into how an application behaves under normal and malicious conditions, revealing security issues that may be missed by other testing methods.

DAST works by interacting with a deployed application through its front-end interface, typically using automated scanners that mimic the actions of a malicious user. These scanners send a variety of inputs, requests, and payloads to the application, looking for signs of security weaknesses such as injection flaws, cross-site scripting, insecure redirects, authentication bypasses, and session management issues. The strength of DAST lies in its ability to see how the entire application stack—including web servers, APIs, and back-end services—responds to unexpected or malformed input. This runtime perspective allows DAST to uncover configuration problems, server-side logic errors, and security missteps that are difficult or impossible to detect through static analysis alone.

One of the primary advantages of DAST is its language-agnostic nature. Since it tests applications from the outside, it does not depend on the programming language or framework used to build the software. This makes DAST a versatile choice for organizations that manage diverse technology stacks or integrate components written in different languages. DAST tools are also well suited for applications that use third-party components or services, as they can identify how external dependencies behave in the context of the application and whether they introduce any vulnerabilities when integrated. For security teams managing large portfolios of applications, DAST provides a scalable way to perform consistent, repeatable security assessments across a wide range of systems.

Integrating DAST into the development pipeline can significantly enhance the security posture of an organization. By automating dynamic testing as part of the CI/CD workflow, teams can detect vulnerabilities as soon as new code is deployed to a test environment. This allows developers to receive timely feedback, address issues early, and prevent insecure releases from reaching production. When configured to run regularly, DAST becomes a continuous validation tool that monitors for regressions, confirms the effectiveness of security controls, and ensures that new features do not introduce new risks. In environments where software is released frequently, such as with agile or DevOps practices, this continuous assessment is critical for maintaining security at speed.

To be effective, DAST tools must be carefully configured and tuned to the application being tested. A poorly configured scanner can generate a high volume of false positives or miss important vulnerabilities altogether. Selecting appropriate scan profiles, customizing payloads, and defining authentication flows are all necessary steps to ensure accurate results. Many applications require login credentials or session tokens to access protected functionality, and DAST tools must be able to handle these authentication mechanisms in order to provide full coverage. Capturing and replaying login sequences, handling token renewal, and navigating complex user flows are important capabilities for any modern DAST tool.

Another critical aspect of DAST is its ability to identify vulnerabilities that arise from the interaction between different components of an application. For example, a DAST scan might reveal that a seemingly harmless endpoint can be manipulated to expose sensitive data or escalate privileges when combined with another action. This type of insight is particularly valuable in microservices architectures and complex web applications, where vulnerabilities often emerge from the way components communicate rather than from individual weaknesses. By observing the live behavior of the application, DAST can detect chaining attacks and unexpected outcomes that might not be apparent in isolated code analysis.

DAST also plays a vital role in validating the effectiveness of other security controls. For example, if an application claims to sanitize user input to prevent cross-site scripting, a DAST scan can test whether this control actually works in practice. If input is still being rendered unsafely in the browser, the scan will detect it. Similarly, DAST can confirm whether authentication systems prevent unauthorized access, whether session expiration behaves as expected, and whether error messages reveal sensitive information. These real-world tests help verify that implemented security measures are not only present but functioning correctly under stress and edge cases.

In addition to automated scanning, DAST can be complemented by manual testing performed by skilled security professionals. Human testers can go beyond the capabilities of automated tools by exploring business logic flaws, abuse cases, and application-specific vulnerabilities. While automation is essential for coverage and scalability, manual testing brings creativity and contextual awareness that machines cannot match. Together, automated DAST and manual testing provide a comprehensive approach to dynamic security assessment, identifying both common and subtle weaknesses in the application.

One challenge associated with DAST is managing the impact of testing on live systems. Because DAST interacts with the application in real time, it can cause unintended behavior, such as triggering alerts, modifying data, or generating excessive load. For this reason, DAST is typically run in staging or pre-production environments that mirror production but are isolated from real users and sensitive data. Careful scheduling and monitoring of scans are important to avoid performance degradation or service disruption. In some cases, production testing may be performed with restricted scan scopes and safety settings, but this requires a thorough understanding of the risks and protections involved.

Reporting and remediation workflows are also key to making the most of DAST. The output from DAST tools should be integrated into issue tracking systems so that developers can triage and resolve findings without leaving their familiar environments. Reports should include clear descriptions of each vulnerability, steps to reproduce the issue, and guidance on how to fix it. Prioritization is crucial, as not all findings carry the same level of risk. By classifying issues based on severity, exploitability, and impact, security teams can help development teams focus on the most critical problems first and manage technical debt in a sustainable way.

Dynamic Application Security Testing provides invaluable insights into how applications behave in real-world scenarios. It reveals vulnerabilities that cannot be detected through static analysis or code review alone and validates the effectiveness of security measures in practice. When integrated into DevSecOps pipelines, DAST enhances visibility, shortens feedback loops, and strengthens collaboration between security and development teams. It is a vital component of any modern application security program, enabling organizations to build, test, and deploy software that is not only functional and scalable but resilient against ever-evolving threats.

Software Composition Analysis (SCA)

Software Composition Analysis, or SCA, has become an essential part of modern application security due to the widespread use of open-source and third-party components in software development. In today's fast-paced development environments, teams rely heavily on external libraries, frameworks, and modules to accelerate delivery and avoid reinventing the wheel. While this approach provides significant benefits in terms of speed and innovation, it also introduces substantial security risks. Many of these dependencies may contain known vulnerabilities, outdated code, or licensing issues that, if left unaddressed, can expose applications to exploitation and compliance failures. SCA helps organizations manage these risks by automatically identifying the components used in their applications, checking them against known vulnerability databases, and providing actionable insights for remediation.

SCA tools work by scanning an application's codebase, build files, and dependencies to create an inventory of all third-party software components and their versions. This includes direct dependencies explicitly referenced in the application as well as transitive dependencies that are pulled in indirectly. Once this software bill of materials is established, the tool compares each component against public vulnerability databases such as the National Vulnerability Database (NVD), GitHub Security Advisories, and vendor-specific alerts. If a component is found to have a known vulnerability, the tool flags it and typically provides information about the severity, CVE identifier, affected versions, and recommended updates or mitigations.

One of the key strengths of Software Composition Analysis is its ability to surface risks that might otherwise remain hidden. Many development teams are unaware of how deeply embedded some vulnerable components can be, particularly when dealing with transitive dependencies. For example, a popular library might depend on another module that has not been maintained in years and contains critical security flaws. Without SCA, these hidden dependencies can silently compromise the security of the entire application. SCA tools give teams the visibility they need to identify and manage these risks proactively.

SCA also plays a critical role in maintaining compliance with software licenses. Open-source components are governed by a variety of licenses, each with its own set of obligations and restrictions. Some licenses may require attribution, others may impose constraints on commercial use, and others may enforce copyleft provisions that demand derivative works also be open-sourced. Using components with incompatible or restrictive licenses can lead to legal complications and reputational damage. SCA tools help organizations track and manage license usage, flagging any potential issues and enabling legal teams to ensure that software distribution complies with internal and external requirements.

The integration of SCA into the DevSecOps pipeline is essential for making vulnerability management a continuous process. SCA tools can be incorporated into continuous integration systems so that every build is automatically scanned for new or existing risks. This provides developers with real-time feedback and prevents vulnerable components from being introduced into the main codebase. Some tools also support policy enforcement, allowing organizations to define rules around acceptable license types or maximum vulnerability severity. If a build violates these rules, it can be automatically blocked until the issues are resolved, ensuring that security and compliance standards are upheld without manual intervention.

Choosing the right SCA tool depends on several factors, including the programming languages used, the complexity of the dependency tree, the level of integration required, and the type of reporting needed. Some tools offer deep integrations with development environments, allowing developers to view and resolve issues directly from their IDE. Others provide advanced analytics and dashboards for security teams to monitor trends, prioritize efforts, and demonstrate compliance. The best tools offer a combination of automation, accuracy, and usability, enabling both developers and security professionals to collaborate effectively on managing software risks.

A common challenge in implementing SCA is managing the volume of findings. Large applications may include hundreds or even thousands of dependencies, many of which have reported vulnerabilities. Not all of these pose immediate or significant risk. Some may be unreachable in the application context, mitigated by configuration, or only exploitable under very specific conditions. Effective SCA requires mechanisms for prioritization, filtering, and triage. Modern tools often use machine learning, exploitability scores, and contextual analysis to help teams focus on the vulnerabilities that matter most. They may also provide remediation advice, such as upgrade paths, patches, or alternative libraries that can be adopted to eliminate the risk.

SCA also contributes to the principle of shift-left security, allowing vulnerabilities to be identified during the earliest phases of development. When developers are made aware of risks as they add new dependencies or update versions, they can make informed choices about whether to proceed, seek alternatives, or update more securely. This proactive approach not only reduces the cost and effort of fixing vulnerabilities later but also fosters a culture of accountability and ownership for security within development teams. Teams begin to understand the implications of their dependency choices and take more care in curating the components they include in their projects.

Beyond immediate vulnerability detection, SCA provides long-term strategic value by establishing a clear inventory of the software supply chain. This visibility becomes especially important during incident response. When a new critical vulnerability is announced in a widely used library, security teams can quickly search across their codebases to identify which applications are affected and initiate remediation. Without an SCA tool and an up-to-date software bill of materials, this process can take days or weeks, leaving systems exposed and organizations unable to respond quickly.

The role of Software Composition Analysis has gained even more prominence with the rise of software supply chain attacks. Threat actors increasingly target third-party components, inserting malicious code into popular libraries or compromising the distribution process itself. High-profile incidents have demonstrated that even trusted packages can be weaponized. SCA, when combined with other supply chain security practices such as code signing, vulnerability disclosure programs, and dependency pinning, becomes a critical layer of defense. It allows organizations to detect anomalies, verify the integrity of components, and enforce strict sourcing policies.

Software Composition Analysis is not a luxury but a necessity in the modern software landscape. It addresses one of the most significant sources of risk in application development—third-party code—and equips teams with the tools they need to manage that risk intelligently. By integrating SCA into every phase of the software lifecycle, from design to deployment, organizations can reduce their exposure to vulnerabilities, maintain legal compliance, and build more secure, resilient, and trustworthy applications. As the reliance on open-source software continues to grow, the importance of SCA will only increase, making it a cornerstone of any effective DevSecOps program.

Container Security Basics

Container security has become a critical area of focus in modern software development and deployment, especially as organizations embrace microservices, DevOps, and cloud-native architectures. Containers offer speed, portability, and scalability by packaging applications with all their dependencies into lightweight, isolated units that can run consistently across different environments. However, the very features that make containers so powerful also introduce new security challenges. Understanding the basics of container security is essential for ensuring that these systems remain protected from vulnerabilities, misconfigurations, and attacks throughout their lifecycle.

At the heart of container security is the need to protect the container image, which serves as the blueprint for container instances. A container image includes the application code, libraries, runtime, configuration files, and any other dependencies required to run the application. If the image contains insecure components, outdated libraries, or malicious code, every container launched from that image will inherit those risks. Securing the image begins with minimizing its contents. This means using base images that are stripped of unnecessary tools and packages, reducing the attack surface and eliminating potential vulnerabilities. Developers should choose official or verified images from trusted registries and avoid downloading random or unverified images from public sources.

Another essential practice is to scan container images regularly for known vulnerabilities. Just as software composition analysis helps identify insecure dependencies in application code, container scanning tools analyze image contents against vulnerability databases. These scans should occur at multiple stages, including during development, build, and deployment, to ensure that new issues are not introduced and existing ones are identified quickly. Scanning should be automated as part of the CI/CD pipeline, with policies in place to prevent the use of images containing high-severity vulnerabilities. In some cases, it may be necessary to rebuild or patch base images as new CVEs are disclosed, requiring a consistent process for image maintenance.

Once a container is running, runtime security becomes the next focus. Containers share the host operating system kernel, which means that a compromise in one container can potentially affect others if proper isolation is not maintained. To mitigate this risk, container runtimes and orchestrators like Docker and Kubernetes offer a variety of security features. One of the foundational controls is the use of namespaces and control groups (cgroups) to isolate processes, memory, and resources between containers. Additionally, containers should be run with the least privilege necessary. This includes avoiding the use of the root user inside containers unless absolutely required, as root privileges inside a container can be exploited to escape the container environment or access host resources.

Implementing security policies through tools like AppArmor or SELinux adds another layer of control over what actions a containerized process can perform. These mandatory access control systems enforce rules that restrict file access, network communication, and process execution based on defined security profiles. When properly configured, they can prevent containers from reading sensitive files, making unauthorized network connections, or executing malicious binaries. For Kubernetes environments, tools like PodSecurityPolicies or the newer Pod Security Standards help define and enforce security requirements at the cluster level, ensuring that deployed containers comply with organizational policies.

Network security is also a crucial aspect of container security. Containers often communicate with each other and with external systems over the network, making it important to control and monitor these interactions. Network segmentation should be implemented to restrict traffic between services based on necessity. Kubernetes network policies can define rules that allow or deny traffic between pods, enforcing the principle of least privilege in service communication. Additionally, all external traffic should be encrypted using TLS to prevent eavesdropping and tampering. Observability tools can provide insights into network activity, helping to detect anomalies such as unexpected traffic flows or potential lateral movement by attackers.

The container lifecycle also includes the orchestration and deployment layers, which must be secured alongside individual containers. Kubernetes, the most widely used container orchestration platform, introduces its own set of security considerations. The Kubernetes API server must be protected with authentication and role-based access control to prevent unauthorized changes to the cluster. Secrets management within Kubernetes must be handled carefully, as secrets stored in plaintext or exposed through environment variables can be easily compromised. Integrating external secret management tools, such as HashiCorp Vault or cloud provider services, provides a more secure and auditable method of storing sensitive information.

Logging and monitoring are essential for detecting and responding to container security incidents. Logs should capture relevant information from both the host and the container environment, including system calls, network connections, file changes, and user actions. Centralized logging systems make it easier to analyze trends, correlate events, and investigate potential breaches. Runtime threat detection tools can monitor container activity for indicators of compromise, such as abnormal system calls, process behavior, or file access patterns. Alerts generated by these tools allow security teams to respond quickly to potential threats and contain incidents before they escalate.

Image signing and verification provide an additional mechanism for ensuring the integrity of container images. By signing images at build time and verifying those signatures at deployment, organizations can ensure that only trusted images are allowed to run in production. This process, supported by tools like Docker Content Trust and Notary, helps prevent tampering and unauthorized changes to container images. Combined with image provenance tracking and immutable infrastructure practices, this strengthens the overall security posture and reduces the chances of supply chain attacks.

Container security also requires an understanding of the underlying host systems. While containers provide process-level isolation, they still rely on the host operating system for many core functions. Therefore, securing the host is just as important as securing the containers themselves. Hosts should be hardened using minimal operating systems designed for container workloads, such as Container-Optimized OS or Bottlerocket. Regular patching, limited access, and intrusion detection systems help protect the host from becoming a target or a launchpad for attacks on other containers.

As containerized applications become more prevalent in production environments, security must evolve to meet the challenges of this dynamic and complex ecosystem. Developers, security engineers, and operations teams must work together to build secure images, configure safe runtime environments, enforce network boundaries, and monitor continuously for threats. Container security is not a single action but an ongoing process that spans the entire lifecycle of development, deployment, and operation. Understanding the fundamentals is the first step toward implementing robust protections and ensuring that containers deliver on their promise of agility, scalability, and resilience without compromising safety.

Securing Docker and Kubernetes

Securing Docker and Kubernetes is a foundational component of any modern DevSecOps strategy. These technologies have transformed the way applications are built, deployed, and scaled, offering unprecedented flexibility and efficiency. However, their dynamic and distributed nature introduces complex security challenges that require careful planning, continuous monitoring, and the implementation of layered defense mechanisms. Ensuring the security of Docker containers and Kubernetes clusters involves protecting every layer of the stack—from the images and containers to the orchestration layer and underlying infrastructure.

Docker, as a containerization platform, enables developers to package applications with their dependencies into portable units. While this approach streamlines development and deployment, it also requires diligence in image management. A secure Docker environment begins with building minimal, clean, and trusted images. Using official or verified base images from trusted sources helps reduce the risk of inheriting known vulnerabilities. Custom images should be built with only the necessary libraries and binaries to reduce the attack surface. Dockerfiles must be written with care, avoiding the use of unnecessary privileges and avoiding the inclusion of secrets, such as credentials or API keys.

Image scanning is a vital part of Docker security. Before containers are deployed, images must be scanned for known vulnerabilities using tools that analyze them against public databases. This scanning should be automated as part of the CI/CD pipeline, ensuring that only secure images are promoted to production. Even after deployment, continuous monitoring of image vulnerabilities is necessary since new threats emerge regularly. When critical vulnerabilities are found, images must be rebuilt using patched versions of dependencies, and affected containers should be replaced promptly.

Another critical aspect of Docker security is the enforcement of the principle of least privilege. Containers should not run as the root user unless absolutely necessary. Granting containers unnecessary privileges can lead to privilege escalation and potential host compromise. Docker provides capabilities such as user namespaces and security profiles using AppArmor or SELinux, which allow teams to restrict the behavior of containerized applications. These profiles can define what files a container can access, what system calls it can make, and what network resources it can use, reducing the potential damage if a container is compromised.

Kubernetes, as a container orchestration platform, adds an additional layer of complexity and responsibility. Securing Kubernetes starts with securing the control plane, which includes components like the API server, etcd, controller manager, and scheduler. The API server is the front door to the Kubernetes cluster, and it must be protected with strict authentication and authorization controls. Role-based access control (RBAC) must be configured to ensure that users and service accounts only have the permissions they need. Administrative privileges should be tightly restricted and regularly audited. Network policies should be applied to control traffic between pods, enforcing the principle of least privilege for inter-service communication.

The Kubernetes etcd datastore, which stores cluster state and secrets, must be encrypted and access-controlled. If attackers gain access to etcd, they can view or alter the configuration of the entire cluster. Transport layer security (TLS) should be used to encrypt all communication between Kubernetes components. Certificates must be managed carefully and rotated regularly to prevent unauthorized access. Additionally, Kubernetes audit logging should be enabled to track API activity, providing visibility into changes and helping with incident investigations.

Pod security is another essential consideration. Kubernetes allows fine-grained control over how pods are configured and what permissions they have. Pod Security Standards or tools like OPA Gatekeeper can be used to enforce policies that prevent dangerous configurations, such as running containers as root, enabling host networking, or mounting sensitive host paths. These policies help ensure that workloads comply with organizational security requirements and reduce the likelihood of accidental misconfigurations that expose the cluster to risk.

Secrets management in Kubernetes also requires careful attention. By default, Kubernetes stores secrets as base64-encoded strings in etcd, which is not secure on its own. Clusters should be configured to encrypt secrets at rest and restrict access to only those services that require them. Integrating with external secret management systems like HashiCorp Vault or cloud-native secrets managers offers a more secure and scalable approach. These systems provide capabilities such as dynamic secrets, access control policies, and auditing, which enhance the overall security of sensitive data within the cluster.

Kubernetes nodes, which are the machines that run container workloads, must also be hardened. Running a minimal operating system designed for containers reduces the attack surface. Nodes should be patched regularly, monitored for unusual activity, and protected by host-based firewalls. Access to the nodes should be limited, preferably through bastion hosts or VPNs, and SSH access should be controlled through identity-based authentication. Container runtime security is also critical, as vulnerabilities in the container runtime, such as Docker or containerd, can allow attackers to escape containers or gain elevated privileges.

Monitoring and logging are crucial components of securing Docker and Kubernetes environments. Centralized logging solutions should collect logs from containers, nodes, and Kubernetes components, providing real-time visibility into system behavior. Security information and event management (SIEM) systems can analyze these logs for suspicious patterns and alert teams to potential threats. Similarly, runtime security tools can observe the behavior of containers and alert on or block anomalous activities such as unexpected file access, process execution, or network communication. These tools provide critical insight into what is happening inside containers and help detect breaches that traditional perimeter defenses might miss.

Enforcing policy and governance at scale is another important dimension of Kubernetes security. As clusters grow and teams adopt GitOps or Infrastructure as Code practices, security policies must be codified and automatically enforced. Tools like Kyverno or OPA

Gatekeeper allow organizations to define custom policies that govern how resources are deployed. For example, policies can require that images come from approved registries, prevent containers from running with privileged access, or enforce resource limits on workloads. These policies ensure consistency and compliance across environments without relying on manual reviews.

Securing Docker and Kubernetes is not a one-time activity but an ongoing process that evolves with the application, the platform, and the threat landscape. It requires close collaboration between development, operations, and security teams. By implementing layered security controls, adopting secure defaults, monitoring continuously, and automating enforcement, organizations can mitigate risks and ensure that their containerized environments remain resilient. As more mission-critical applications move into Kubernetes, the security of these environments becomes a defining factor in the overall trust and success of software systems. Understanding and applying the fundamentals of Docker and Kubernetes security is essential for any team building and deploying software in a cloud-native world.

Infrastructure as Code (IaC) Security

Infrastructure as Code, commonly referred to as IaC, has revolutionized the way organizations provision and manage their IT environments. By treating infrastructure configuration as code, teams can automate the deployment of servers, networks, databases, storage, and other components in a repeatable, consistent, and scalable manner. Tools such as Terraform, AWS CloudFormation, Ansible, and Pulumi allow developers and operations teams to define infrastructure using declarative or imperative code stored in version control systems. This approach brings the benefits of speed, transparency, and collaboration to infrastructure management, but it also introduces a new category of security risks that must be addressed with the same level of attention as application code. IaC security is no longer optional—it is a core requirement for organizations seeking to secure their cloud-native environments.

The adoption of IaC shifts the responsibility for security controls into the development process. Infrastructure configurations, once managed manually by system administrators, are now embedded into CI/CD pipelines and subject to rapid iteration. This transformation means that misconfigurations and security vulnerabilities can be introduced at the same pace as application code. An improperly configured security group, a publicly accessible storage bucket, or a disabled encryption setting can all become part of the automated infrastructure and be deployed instantly across environments. Such issues are often not the result of malicious intent, but of oversight, lack of visibility, or insufficient knowledge of secure configuration practices.

One of the foundational principles of IaC security is the early detection of misconfigurations through automated scanning. Just as static analysis tools evaluate application code for security vulnerabilities, specialized IaC scanning tools inspect infrastructure code for unsafe practices. These tools parse configuration files and check them against a set of security policies and best practices. They can identify whether resources are exposed to the public internet, whether data encryption is enforced, whether identity and access management settings are too permissive, or whether logging and monitoring are properly configured. Running these checks during the development phase allows teams to catch and fix issues before they are deployed, reducing the risk of introducing vulnerabilities into production environments.

Integrating IaC security scanning into the CI/CD pipeline ensures that every change to infrastructure code is automatically evaluated before it is merged or deployed. This continuous validation process supports the DevSecOps goal of shifting security left and promotes a culture of accountability among developers and DevOps engineers. Security no longer acts as a gatekeeper that slows down deployment but becomes a built-in part of the workflow. Policy-as-code tools such as Open Policy Agent and Sentinel allow organizations to define custom rules that align with their internal standards, enabling automated enforcement of complex requirements. For example, a policy can block any pull request that attempts to create a storage bucket without server-side encryption or a virtual machine without a secure firewall.

Version control is another critical aspect of IaC security. By keeping infrastructure code in source repositories, organizations gain visibility into the history of changes, who made them, and why. This audit trail is invaluable for both troubleshooting and compliance. Code reviews provide an opportunity to catch security issues, validate intentions, and ensure adherence to policies. Peer reviews help build a shared understanding of secure configurations and foster collaboration across teams. Version-controlled infrastructure also enables rollback capabilities, allowing teams to revert to a known good state if a misconfiguration is introduced.

Secrets management is a particularly sensitive area in IaC security. It is essential that secrets such as API keys, passwords, and private keys are never hardcoded into infrastructure files. Including secrets in code repositories, even private ones, can lead to unintentional exposure and compromise. Instead, secrets should be managed through secure vaults or secret management services that provide access control, auditing, and dynamic credentials. Integration between IaC tools and secret management systems helps enforce this separation and reduces the likelihood of accidental leaks.

Role-based access control and the principle of least privilege must also extend to IaC practices. Not all users need the ability to apply changes to production infrastructure. Access to infrastructure code repositories and deployment tools should be carefully controlled based on roles and responsibilities. Sensitive actions such as modifying firewall rules, changing encryption settings, or managing credentials should be limited to authorized individuals and subject to approval processes. Logs of access and changes should be maintained and reviewed regularly to detect unauthorized activity or policy violations.

Environment segregation further strengthens IaC security. Development, staging, and production environments should be isolated, with separate state files, variables, and access controls. This separation minimizes the risk of accidental deployment to the wrong environment and helps contain the blast radius of potential misconfigurations. IaC tools support environment-specific configurations, allowing teams to tailor security settings appropriately. For example, logging and monitoring may be more extensive in production, while broader access controls may be acceptable in development for testing purposes.

Drift detection is another important concept in maintaining IaC security. Over time, changes may be made directly to live environments outside of the IaC workflow, whether intentionally or accidentally. This creates configuration drift, where the actual infrastructure no longer matches the declared code. Drift can lead to unpredictable behavior, hidden vulnerabilities, and compliance issues. Regular scans and reconciliation processes help detect drift and ensure that infrastructure remains in a desired, secure state. Some tools allow for automated remediation, where the infrastructure is automatically realigned with the IaC definition when discrepancies are found.

Monitoring and observability are vital for IaC security beyond the initial deployment. Infrastructure must be continuously monitored for changes, anomalies, and threats. Telemetry data from cloud providers, logs from IaC tools, and alerts from security scanners should feed into a centralized monitoring system. This data allows security teams to detect unusual patterns, investigate incidents, and respond quickly to misconfigurations or attacks. Integrating infrastructure monitoring with incident response tools further enhances an organization's ability to manage security events effectively.

As infrastructure becomes increasingly dynamic and ephemeral, the role of code in defining and controlling infrastructure grows in importance. Security must evolve alongside these practices, embracing automation, policy enforcement, and proactive monitoring. Infrastructure as Code offers a powerful opportunity to codify not only system configurations but also the security principles that protect them. By embedding security into every phase of the IaC lifecycle, organizations can reduce risk, improve resilience, and maintain control over their infrastructure in an ever-changing digital landscape.

Secrets Management Best Practices

In the modern landscape of cloud-native applications, continuous deployment, and microservices, secrets management has become a cornerstone of secure system architecture. Secrets refer to sensitive data such as API keys, passwords, tokens, encryption keys, SSH credentials, and certificates that are used to authenticate users, systems, and services. These elements are essential for system operation, but when mishandled, they can lead to severe security breaches, unauthorized access, and compromised infrastructure. The challenges of secrets management are amplified in environments where infrastructure is defined as code, applications scale dynamically, and automated pipelines push changes into production at high velocity. Managing secrets securely and efficiently requires a disciplined approach supported by robust tooling, policies, and cultural awareness.

One of the most critical best practices in secrets management is to never hardcode secrets directly into source code. This is one of the most common and dangerous mistakes in software development. Secrets embedded in code are easily exposed through version control systems, code sharing, and misconfigured repositories. Once committed, a secret can remain in the version history indefinitely, even if removed in later commits. Attackers often scan public repositories for these kinds of secrets, using automated tools to extract credentials and gain unauthorized access. To mitigate this risk, developers must be trained to separate secrets from application logic and use secure references instead.

Storing secrets in environment variables is a common pattern, but it must be approached with caution. While environment variables provide a way to inject secrets at runtime without storing them in code, they can still be exposed if not handled properly. Processes that crash or generate verbose logs may accidentally expose their environment, and misconfigured access permissions can allow unauthorized users to view them. For higher security assurance, secrets should be managed using a dedicated secrets management system. These platforms are designed specifically to store, encrypt, audit, and control access to sensitive data.

Secrets management tools such as HashiCorp Vault, AWS Secrets Manager, Azure Key Vault, and Google Secret Manager provide centralized solutions for managing sensitive information. These tools encrypt secrets at rest and in transit, enforce fine-grained access controls, and offer comprehensive audit logging. They can also rotate secrets automatically, a best practice that reduces the window of opportunity for attackers who manage to obtain a credential. Secret rotation ensures that credentials are regularly refreshed and outdated secrets are revoked, minimizing the blast radius of a potential compromise. Automation plays a vital role in managing rotations without introducing downtime or disruption to dependent services.

Access control is another core aspect of effective secrets management. Not every user, service, or process needs access to all secrets. Implementing the principle of least privilege means that entities are granted access only to the secrets they need to perform their tasks. Role-based access control or attribute-based access control policies can be used to define who can read, write, or manage specific secrets. Integration with identity providers and enforcement of authentication requirements adds an additional layer of security. For example, secrets access can be restricted to specific machines, services, or authenticated users with valid tokens, further reducing the risk of misuse.

Auditability and visibility are crucial in managing secrets at scale. A secure system should be able to track who accessed which secret, when, and from where. This audit trail provides accountability and helps organizations identify suspicious behavior. If a breach occurs, logs can be used to reconstruct events and understand the scope of the compromise. Most secrets managers support detailed logging and monitoring, and these logs should be integrated into a centralized logging or SIEM platform for analysis and alerting. Monitoring for anomalous access patterns, such as repeated failed attempts or access from unusual locations, enables early detection of potential threats.

Encryption is the foundation upon which all secrets management relies. Secrets should never be stored in plaintext, whether in a file, a database, or in memory. Industry-standard encryption algorithms must be used, and the encryption keys themselves must be protected using hardware security modules or cloud-based key management systems. Double encryption, where data is encrypted both by the secrets manager and by the storage layer, can provide defense in depth. Secure key lifecycle management, including generation, storage, usage, and destruction, must be implemented and regularly reviewed to ensure that encryption remains effective and compliant with organizational and regulatory requirements.

In dynamic environments such as Kubernetes, secrets management introduces additional complexities. Kubernetes offers native secret management via its Secret resources, but by default, these are stored in etcd as base64-encoded strings, which does not constitute proper encryption. Best practices include enabling encryption at rest for etcd, restricting access to Kubernetes secrets through RBAC, and integrating Kubernetes with external secrets managers. Using tools like External Secrets Operator allows secrets to be pulled securely from cloud vaults and injected into pods at runtime without being stored permanently in the cluster.

Application design must also consider secure secret usage. Secrets should be loaded at runtime and held in memory for as little time as possible. Avoid logging secrets or sending them over unsecured channels. When integrating with third-party APIs, credentials should be scoped appropriately. For example, API tokens should have read-only access when write access is not required, and time-limited tokens should be preferred over long-lived ones. Implementing retry logic and graceful error handling ensures that secret access failures do not cascade into service outages.

As part of a DevSecOps culture, secrets management must be integrated into the development lifecycle and deployment processes. Secrets should be treated as first class entities with the same rigor as code or infrastructure. They should be reviewed, tested, and managed through automated workflows. Policies regarding secret creation, rotation, expiration, and revocation should be documented and enforced consistently. Continuous training and awareness are vital, as human error remains a leading cause of secret leaks. Development and operations teams must be equipped with knowledge and tools that promote secure behavior by default.

Effective secrets management is both a technical and organizational challenge. It requires the right tools, the right processes, and the right mindset. As systems grow in complexity and automation becomes pervasive, the volume and sensitivity of secrets will only increase. Mismanagement can have devastating consequences, from service disruptions to full-scale data breaches. By adopting best practices, enforcing strict controls, and integrating security at every layer, organizations can maintain trust in their systems and protect the confidentiality, integrity, and availability of their applications and data.

Identity and Access Management (IAM) in DevSecOps

Identity and Access Management, commonly known as IAM, plays a foundational role in the security framework of any DevSecOps environment. As organizations embrace agile development cycles, cloud infrastructure, and automation, the number of users, systems, services, and machines interacting within the ecosystem grows exponentially. Each of these entities must be properly identified, authenticated, and authorized to perform only the actions they are allowed to. IAM provides the policies, processes, and technologies that ensure only the right individuals and components have the appropriate level of access to critical systems and data, and it enforces these permissions consistently across the development, testing, and production environments. In the context of DevSecOps, where security is embedded into every stage of the software lifecycle, IAM becomes a critical enabler for maintaining both speed and security.

IAM in DevSecOps begins with the principle of identity centralization. Every user, service, and device must have a unique identity that can be authenticated and monitored. Without centralized identity, access decisions become fragmented and inconsistent, increasing the likelihood of privilege creep, misconfigurations, and gaps in security coverage. Identity providers such as LDAP directories, cloud-based identity services, and federated identity platforms offer a single source of truth for user and service identities. Integrating these systems with access control mechanisms ensures that policies are applied uniformly across environments, regardless of whether they are on-premises, in the cloud, or in hybrid infrastructures.

Authentication, the process of verifying an entity's identity, must be robust and resistant to compromise. Multi-factor authentication is a fundamental requirement for any system with sensitive access, adding a second layer of protection beyond usernames and passwords.

DevSecOps teams should implement strong authentication mechanisms for developers, administrators, and CI/CD systems that interact with infrastructure or deploy code. Service accounts and non-human identities, which are often overlooked, also require secure authentication through cryptographic keys, certificates, or short-lived tokens issued by trusted identity providers. The use of ephemeral credentials instead of static secrets significantly reduces the risk of leaked or compromised access.

Authorization, which defines what an authenticated identity is allowed to do, is equally important. Role-based access control, or RBAC, is a widely used model where permissions are grouped by role, and identities are assigned roles based on their responsibilities. This model simplifies access management and auditing by abstracting individual permissions into broader categories. In DevSecOps, RBAC ensures that developers, testers, and operators can only perform actions relevant to their duties. For instance, a developer may be permitted to push code to a repository or initiate a test pipeline, but not to modify production infrastructure or access sensitive logs. Security policies should reflect the principle of least privilege, which states that identities should be granted the minimum level of access necessary to complete their tasks.

To enhance flexibility and precision, attribute-based access control can be used in more advanced IAM implementations. In ABAC, access decisions are made based on a combination of attributes such as user role, time of access, location, or the sensitivity level of a resource. This allows for fine-grained policies that can adapt to dynamic environments, such as restricting access to production systems outside business hours or granting temporary elevated privileges during incident response. In the fast-changing world of DevSecOps, where infrastructure and team roles can evolve rapidly, such adaptability is essential for maintaining strong security while supporting operational agility.

One of the challenges in IAM for DevSecOps is managing the proliferation of identities, especially those belonging to automated systems. CI/CD pipelines, build servers, cloud automation tools, and monitoring agents all require access to various resources. These machine identities must be managed with the same discipline as human users. Their credentials should be stored securely, rotated regularly, and scoped as narrowly as possible. Tools that support machine identity management and integrate with secrets managers help streamline this process. Temporary credentials issued via identity providers or access brokers provide enhanced security and reduce the window of exposure in case of compromise.

Auditability and observability are key features of effective IAM in DevSecOps. Every access attempt, whether successful or denied, should be logged and monitored. These logs must be centralized and analyzed for anomalies, such as failed login attempts, unauthorized access, or privilege escalation. Integrating IAM logs into a SIEM platform or security monitoring tool enables real-time detection of suspicious activity and supports forensic investigations in case of incidents. Regular reviews of access logs, especially for privileged accounts and critical systems, help identify patterns that might suggest insider threats or misconfigurations.

IAM must also be embedded into the development lifecycle. This includes defining and enforcing access policies in code, versioning them alongside infrastructure definitions, and integrating access controls into CI/CD workflows. For example, policies can be defined that prevent deployments unless access conditions are met, such as code approvals or successful security scans. Policy-as-code frameworks allow organizations to express IAM rules in a programmatic, testable, and reusable format. This codification aligns with the DevSecOps principle of automation and supports compliance with security and regulatory standards.

Cloud-native environments bring additional considerations for IAM. Each cloud provider has its own IAM model and set of services, such as AWS IAM, Azure Active Directory, or Google Cloud IAM. These services allow fine-grained control over resources and support integrations with enterprise identity providers. When using multi-cloud or hybrid environments, consistency becomes a challenge. Teams must ensure that access policies are harmonized across platforms and that identities can be federated or mapped securely. Cloud IAM roles and policies should be reviewed regularly, and automated tools can be used to detect overly permissive or orphaned roles that pose a security risk.

Training and culture play a critical role in IAM success within DevSecOps. All team members must understand the importance of managing access securely and the potential risks of misconfigurations or credential leaks. Security champions within development and operations teams can help promote best practices and act as local points of expertise. Continuous education, simulated phishing exercises, and red team assessments can reinforce awareness and drive behavior change. IAM is not just a technical mechanism; it is a reflection of how an organization thinks about trust, accountability, and responsibility.

Identity and Access Management in DevSecOps is not a standalone function but a thread that weaves through every phase of the software lifecycle. From securing development environments and enforcing CI/CD pipeline integrity to protecting cloud infrastructure and enabling incident response, IAM provides the foundation for secure, scalable, and resilient systems. It must be automated, observable, and deeply integrated with the tools and practices that drive modern software delivery. As organizations continue to adopt DevSecOps, the ability to manage identity and access effectively will determine their capacity to innovate securely and sustain trust in an increasingly interconnected digital world.

Automating Compliance Checks

Automating compliance checks has become a vital practice in modern DevSecOps environments, where development cycles are fast, infrastructure is dynamic, and regulatory obligations are increasingly complex. Compliance, in this context, refers to the adherence to internal security policies, industry standards, and legal or regulatory frameworks that govern the handling of systems, data, and access controls. Traditional approaches to compliance rely heavily on manual processes, periodic audits, and static documentation. These methods are too slow, error-prone, and reactive to keep up with the pace of today's software development and deployment. Automating compliance shifts the model from one of occasional inspection to one of continuous enforcement, turning compliance into a living, integral part of the development lifecycle.

The value of automated compliance checks lies in their ability to enforce security and policy requirements consistently across environments without human intervention. Whether an organization is subject to external frameworks like GDPR, HIPAA, PCI-DSS, ISO 27001, or follows internal standards for configuration management, access control, and data protection, these rules can be codified and embedded into the infrastructure, application, and deployment workflows. When compliance policies are expressed as code, they become versioned, testable, and auditable, aligning them with the same principles that govern application development in DevSecOps.

One of the key enablers of compliance automation is the policy-as-code model. Policy-as-code allows organizations to define security and compliance requirements in a declarative format, using domain-specific languages or tools that integrate with infrastructure-as-code frameworks and CI/CD pipelines. Tools such as Open Policy Agent, Conftest, Sentinel, and Kyverno enable teams to write policies that enforce rules like denying public access to storage buckets, requiring encryption at rest, or preventing containers from running as root. These policies can be tested automatically against infrastructure definitions during code review or deployment, ensuring that non-compliant configurations are caught before they are applied to production.

Integrating compliance checks into CI/CD pipelines allows teams to identify violations as early as possible. When developers push changes to infrastructure or application configurations, automated tests validate these changes against compliance policies. If a change introduces a violation, the pipeline can be configured to block the deployment and provide feedback to the developer, explaining the nature of the issue and how to fix it. This real-time feedback loop reinforces secure practices and reduces the cost of compliance by eliminating the need for manual checks and rework. Over time, developers internalize these requirements, leading to more secure and compliant code from the outset.

Automated compliance checks also support the principle of continuous compliance. Instead of relying on point-in-time audits, which may miss transient issues or outdated systems, continuous compliance ensures that systems remain aligned with policies at all times. This is achieved by continuously monitoring deployed environments, scanning for deviations from approved baselines, and triggering alerts or remediations when violations are detected. Cloud-native environments, where infrastructure changes frequently and services scale dynamically, benefit immensely from this approach. Tools like AWS Config, Azure Policy, and Google Cloud Config Validator allow organizations to monitor compliance in real time and respond quickly to drift or misconfigurations.

Another major benefit of automating compliance checks is the reduction of audit fatigue. Preparing for audits traditionally requires collecting documentation, assembling evidence, and demonstrating that controls are in place and working. With automation, much of this evidence is generated and collected automatically. Logs of compliance checks, policy evaluations, and access controls can be stored and reviewed at any time, providing auditors with a clear and up-to-date picture of the organization's security posture. This not only simplifies audit preparation but also increases confidence in the integrity of the data and the effectiveness of the controls.

Automating compliance checks also improves visibility across teams and systems. Dashboards and reporting tools can aggregate the results of automated checks, highlighting trends, identifying areas of risk, and tracking remediation progress. These insights help security and compliance teams prioritize their efforts, focus on the most critical issues, and measure the effectiveness of their programs. Transparency also fosters a culture of shared responsibility, where developers, operations, and security professionals all have access to the same data and work collaboratively to maintain compliance.

The process of automating compliance checks requires a shift in mindset and investment in tooling and processes. Organizations must start by identifying the regulations, standards, and internal policies that apply to their systems and translating those requirements into actionable policies. This often involves close collaboration between security, compliance, legal, and engineering teams to ensure that policies are both enforceable and aligned with business goals. Once defined, these policies must be integrated into the development workflow, using automation tools and CI/CD platforms to enforce them consistently and without friction.

Training and cultural change are also critical to the success of compliance automation. Developers must understand the purpose and impact of compliance policies, not just see them as blockers. Security and compliance teams must act as enablers, helping developers write secure code, configure infrastructure properly, and understand how to meet policy requirements. Open communication, clear documentation, and responsive support are essential for building trust and ensuring adoption. When compliance is seen as a shared objective rather than a burden, teams are more likely to engage with the process and take ownership of their responsibilities.

Despite the benefits, automating compliance checks is not without challenges. Policies must be updated as regulations change and environments evolve. Tools must be maintained and configured correctly to ensure accurate evaluations. False positives and overly strict rules can frustrate developers and lead to resistance. To avoid these pitfalls, organizations must adopt a flexible and iterative approach, refining policies over time, soliciting feedback from users, and tuning automation to balance security and productivity.

Ultimately, automating compliance checks transforms compliance from a static, retrospective activity into a dynamic, proactive component of software delivery. It allows organizations to keep pace with regulatory demands, reduce risk, and build trust with customers and stakeholders. In a DevSecOps world, where speed, scale, and security must coexist, compliance automation becomes not only a best practice but a strategic necessity. Through automation, compliance becomes a natural part of the pipeline, enabling teams to innovate securely while meeting the ever-growing expectations of governance, risk management, and regulatory oversight.

Security Gateways in CI/CD Pipelines

Security gateways in CI/CD pipelines are a critical component of modern DevSecOps practices, acting as automated control points that enforce security policies and block the progression of insecure code, misconfigurations, or noncompliant artifacts through the development lifecycle. As organizations adopt continuous integration and continuous delivery models to accelerate software development, the pace of code changes and deployments increases significantly. This speed, while beneficial for innovation and responsiveness, also introduces risk. Without proper checks and balances, insecure code or infrastructure changes can move from development to production in a matter of minutes, potentially exposing systems to vulnerabilities and breaches. Security gateways serve as automated checkpoints within the pipeline, ensuring that security and compliance standards are met before code moves forward.

The concept of security gateways is based on embedding security validation at key stages of the CI/CD pipeline. These validation stages can occur at the commit level, during build and test phases, before deployment to staging, and before promotion to production. Each gateway evaluates the state of the code, the configuration, or the infrastructure definition against a defined set of policies. If the criteria are not met, the pipeline is halted, and feedback is provided to the developer or team responsible. This approach prevents insecure changes from progressing, supports early detection of issues, and promotes a culture of accountability and continuous improvement.

A typical security gateway during the build phase may include static application security testing to scan source code for vulnerabilities. If high severity issues such as injection flaws, insecure deserialization, or broken access controls are detected, the gateway blocks the build from proceeding. Similarly, software composition analysis tools scan dependencies for known vulnerabilities or license violations. If a critical vulnerability is discovered in a third-party library, the gateway prevents the build from advancing until the issue is resolved. This ensures that only code that meets predefined security standards enters later stages of the pipeline.

In the test stage, dynamic application security testing can be used as a gateway to identify runtime vulnerabilities in the application. These tools simulate real-world attacks on a running version of the application in a test environment. If exploitable issues are found, the pipeline can be configured to stop and alert the appropriate team. Security gateways can also evaluate the results of integration and end-to-end tests, ensuring that security features like authentication, authorization, and encryption are functioning as intended. If any security-critical functionality fails validation, deployment is blocked.

Infrastructure as code definitions are also evaluated by security gateways. Tools such as Terraform, CloudFormation, or Kubernetes manifests are scanned using policy-as-code tools like Open Policy Agent or Checkov. These scans verify that infrastructure settings do not violate security policies, such as open security groups, lack of encryption, or improper IAM roles. When a violation is detected, the gateway halts the deployment and provides detailed information on the specific policy breach. This prevents misconfigured infrastructure from being provisioned and reduces the risk of exposing sensitive resources.

Before deployment to production, security gateways can enforce even stricter controls. Container images can be scanned one final time to ensure they are free from critical vulnerabilities and were built from approved base images. Image signing and verification can be checked to confirm provenance and integrity. Configuration files, environment variables, and secrets can be validated to ensure that they are securely managed and not exposed. Deployment manifests are reviewed against compliance checklists to ensure that the application adheres to regulatory standards. Only when all criteria are met does the pipeline allow the deployment to proceed to production.

The strength of security gateways lies in their automation and consistency. Unlike manual reviews, which are subject to human error, security gateways operate with the same rules every time. They scale with the development process and provide immediate feedback to developers, enabling rapid remediation. This shift-left approach ensures that security is addressed during development, not after the fact, reducing the cost and complexity of fixing issues. By integrating these controls directly into the CI/CD pipeline, organizations move from reactive to proactive security, embedding protection into the very fabric of software delivery.

Security gateways must also be flexible and context-aware. Not all security issues are equal, and pipelines should be designed to assess the severity, exploitability, and business impact of findings. Some issues may warrant immediate blocking, while others might allow conditional progression with warnings and tracking. Organizations can define risk tolerance thresholds that align with their business priorities and compliance obligations. For example, a critical vulnerability in a core authentication module may block the pipeline, while a medium-severity issue in a less exposed component may trigger a warning and create a backlog item for later resolution.

Feedback from security gateways should be actionable and integrated into the tools developers already use. Detailed error messages, links to remediation guidance, and access to scan reports empower teams to resolve issues quickly. Integrations with version control systems, ticketing platforms, and collaboration tools ensure that findings are communicated effectively and tracked through resolution. This reduces friction and increases the likelihood that security controls are embraced rather than bypassed.

Implementing effective security gateways requires a collaborative effort between development, operations, and security teams. Security policies must be defined clearly and translated into rules that automation tools can enforce. Teams must agree on acceptable risk levels, remediation procedures, and escalation paths. Tools must be selected and configured to integrate seamlessly with the existing pipeline architecture. Training and documentation must be provided so that all team members understand how the gateways work and how to respond to issues when they arise.

Security gateways also support audit and compliance efforts by generating logs and reports of all validation checks, decisions, and outcomes. These artifacts provide evidence that security controls are consistently applied and enforced throughout the development lifecycle. During audits or incident investigations, these records demonstrate that the organization takes proactive steps to manage risk and comply with regulatory standards. This transparency builds trust with customers, regulators, and stakeholders.

In highly regulated or mission-critical environments, security gateways can be further extended with manual approval gates. These gates require human intervention to review and approve certain changes, such as the deployment of sensitive features or updates to critical infrastructure components. While manual gates reduce automation speed, they provide an additional layer of oversight and accountability when necessary. Combining automated and manual gates allows organizations to tailor their pipelines to meet both speed and security requirements.

Security gateways in CI/CD pipelines are an essential part of any DevSecOps program. They represent the enforcement mechanism for security policies, bridging the gap between rapid software delivery and rigorous risk management. By embedding security checks at each stage of the pipeline, organizations can catch vulnerabilities early, prevent unsafe changes, and ensure that only secure, compliant, and trustworthy applications reach production. As the pace of development continues to accelerate, security gateways ensure that speed does not come at the cost of safety.

Secure Coding Practices

Secure coding practices form the foundation of software that is resilient, trustworthy, and able to withstand real-world threats. In a world where software drives critical infrastructure, manages sensitive data, and powers every aspect of digital life, the quality and security of code cannot be left to chance. Secure coding is not just about fixing bugs or preventing vulnerabilities after they have been discovered—it is about writing software in a way that anticipates risks, mitigates threats, and protects users from the very beginning. It involves a deliberate and disciplined approach to development, where developers are not only focused on functionality and performance but also on confidentiality, integrity, and availability.

One of the most important aspects of secure coding is input validation. Applications often fail when they assume that input from users, external systems, or other sources is safe and predictable. Attackers exploit these assumptions by injecting malicious input designed to manipulate application behavior. Whether it is SQL injection, cross-site scripting, command injection, or path traversal, these attacks rely on poor handling of user input. Secure code treats all input as untrusted until proven otherwise. It validates, sanitizes, and encodes input based on context. Input that is used in SQL queries should be parameterized. Input displayed on web pages should be HTML-encoded. Input used in file paths should be validated for length, characters, and location. These defensive patterns reduce the risk of exploitation and ensure that applications behave securely under unexpected conditions.

Another core principle of secure coding is the principle of least privilege. Code should run with the minimal set of permissions necessary to perform its tasks. If a function only needs to read from a file, it should not be granted write access. If an application component only needs to access a specific database table, it should not have full access to the entire database. This principle extends to APIs, background jobs, third-party integrations, and user roles. By limiting what code can do and what resources it can access, developers reduce the potential impact of a compromise. Even if an attacker exploits a vulnerability, the damage they can do is contained by the restrictions in place.

Error handling and logging also play a significant role in secure coding. Poorly handled errors can crash applications, expose sensitive information, or provide attackers with clues about the underlying system. Secure code uses structured error handling to gracefully manage failures and protect internal details. It logs errors for auditing and debugging but avoids including sensitive data in the logs. For example, stack traces, database queries, authentication tokens, or user credentials should never appear in log files. Logging should be consistent, contextual, and designed to support incident response while preserving confidentiality and integrity.

Authentication and authorization mechanisms must be implemented with care. Developers must never reinvent authentication systems or rely on simplistic schemes like storing plaintext passwords. Passwords should be hashed using strong, adaptive algorithms such as bcrypt or Argon2, with proper salting. Authentication tokens should be time-limited, cryptographically secure, and stored in secure HTTP-only cookies or encrypted local storage. Multi-factor authentication should be implemented wherever feasible. Authorization checks should occur on the server side, not just in the client, and must verify both the user's identity and their permissions for the requested action. Insecure or missing authorization checks can lead to privilege escalation, data leakage, and unauthorized actions.

Dependencies are another area of concern in secure coding. Modern applications rely heavily on open-source libraries and frameworks, which introduce external code into the application. While these dependencies accelerate development, they also introduce risk. Vulnerabilities in third-party components can be exploited by attackers to compromise the application, especially if those dependencies are outdated or poorly maintained. Developers must track their dependencies, monitor them for known vulnerabilities, and update them regularly. Dependency scanning tools can help identify risky components and suggest secure alternatives or patches. Trusting only reputable sources and avoiding unnecessary packages reduces the overall attack surface.

Secure coding also involves managing secrets properly. Secrets such as API keys, encryption keys, database credentials, and tokens must never be hardcoded into source files or stored in version control systems. They should be injected securely at runtime from trusted secret management systems and encrypted both at rest and in transit. Access to secrets should be tightly controlled, audited, and rotated regularly to minimize the risk of exposure. Even in development environments, secure practices should be followed to prevent accidental leaks or misuse.

Concurrency and resource management are often overlooked in secure coding but are essential for building reliable and secure systems. Code that mishandles threads, processes, or memory can lead to race conditions, deadlocks, memory leaks, and denial-of-service conditions. Developers must understand how their code behaves under load and in multi-threaded environments. Using safe concurrency patterns, synchronizing access to shared resources, and managing timeouts and limits are part of writing secure and stable code.

Secure coding also includes protecting data at rest and in transit. Sensitive data should be encrypted using strong, industry-standard algorithms. Data stored in databases, file systems, or backups should be protected from unauthorized access and tampering. Data transmitted over networks must use secure protocols such as HTTPS and TLS, with proper certificate management and validation. Data integrity checks and digital signatures help verify that data has not been altered. Developers should be aware of where sensitive data flows, how it is stored, and who has access to it at every stage of the application lifecycle.

Code review is an important practice that supports secure coding. Peer reviews provide an opportunity to catch security issues that automated tools might miss. Reviewers can assess the logic, structure, and flow of code, asking questions about edge cases, input handling, error management, and access controls. Code reviews also promote shared learning and a culture of continuous improvement. When security is a regular part of code review checklists, it reinforces its importance and normalizes secure thinking among the development team.

Education and awareness are critical for sustaining secure coding practices. Developers must stay informed about evolving threats, new attack techniques, and emerging best practices. Security should be part of onboarding, ongoing training, and daily development work. Organizations should support secure development through resources, tooling, and collaboration with security teams. Developers should be encouraged to ask questions, report concerns, and learn from incidents without fear of blame. A culture that values security and empowers developers to write safe code is the most effective defense against software vulnerabilities.

Secure coding is not a one-time task or a checklist to be completed. It is a mindset, a discipline, and a commitment to building software that is not only functional but trustworthy. Every line of code has the potential to introduce risk or to prevent it. By applying secure coding practices consistently, developers become the first line of defense in protecting users, systems, and data in an increasingly hostile digital world.

DevSecOps in Continuous Integration

DevSecOps in Continuous Integration represents the practical application of security principles at the earliest and most iterative stage of the modern software development lifecycle. Continuous Integration, or CI, is a core component of DevOps, where developers merge code changes frequently into a shared repository. Each integration is verified through automated builds and tests, enabling teams to detect and resolve issues early. In the traditional development model, security reviews and testing often occurred much later, sometimes just before release. This reactive approach led to delays, expensive rework, and in many cases, security vulnerabilities being discovered only after deployment. By embedding security into Continuous Integration, DevSecOps shifts the focus from reactive to proactive, turning security into a continuous, automated, and integrated process.

The integration of DevSecOps into CI begins with automated security checks that are triggered whenever code is committed to the repository. These checks can include static application security testing tools that analyze source code for vulnerabilities such as injection flaws, buffer overflows, and insecure API usage. Developers receive immediate feedback if their code introduces risks, allowing them to fix issues before they become deeply embedded in the project. This real-time feedback loop is crucial for fostering a secure development mindset. It reduces the burden on security teams by catching problems early and empowers developers to take responsibility for the security of their code.

Another fundamental aspect of DevSecOps in CI is dependency management. Modern applications rely heavily on third-party libraries and frameworks, which often contain known vulnerabilities. Software Composition Analysis tools automatically scan project dependencies for Common Vulnerabilities and Exposures and provide detailed reports about which components are affected, their severity, and available fixes. By integrating this scanning into the CI pipeline, teams ensure that any pull request introducing a vulnerable library is flagged before it can be merged. This not only reduces the attack surface but also supports compliance with software supply chain regulations and industry standards.

Code quality tools also play a significant role in maintaining secure coding practices. Linters and static code analyzers enforce style guides and best practices, which indirectly contribute to security by reducing ambiguity and promoting consistency. These tools help developers avoid common pitfalls, encourage the use of safe APIs, and promote maintainable, testable code. When integrated into CI pipelines, they become part of the development routine, creating a seamless experience where quality and security are treated as inseparable aspects of the same workflow.

Configuration files, which often define infrastructure and application behavior, must also be included in the scope of CI security. Infrastructure as Code tools like Terraform and Kubernetes manifests describe environments that can be deployed automatically. If these configurations include insecure defaults, open access rules, or misconfigured storage, they introduce significant risks. Policy-as-code tools integrated into CI can evaluate these files against defined security policies and block insecure changes. This ensures that infrastructure, just like application code, meets organizational standards before it is applied.

Credential management within the CI pipeline is another critical area of focus. Pipelines require access to various resources such as repositories, artifact stores, databases, and cloud services. If these secrets are hardcoded or improperly managed, they can be exposed and abused. Secure CI practices include the use of environment variables, encrypted secret stores, and secret injection mechanisms provided by the CI platform. Access to secrets should be minimized, tightly controlled, and audited. Integrating secret scanning tools into the CI process helps detect credentials that may have been accidentally committed, allowing for immediate mitigation.

Integrating container security into CI is essential for teams using Docker and other container technologies. As part of the pipeline, container images should be built and scanned for vulnerabilities before they are pushed to a registry. These scans examine both the application code and the base image, ensuring that known security flaws are identified early. Image signing and verification processes can also be included, ensuring the integrity and provenance of containers. Only images that pass these checks should be allowed to progress further in the deployment pipeline.

Security testing at the CI level also extends to dynamic elements. While full-scale dynamic application security testing may be more suited to staging or pre-production environments, lightweight dynamic tests can be executed during CI to validate basic security behaviors. These may include checks for common HTTP headers, TLS configurations, or basic authentication responses. Additionally, unit and integration tests should include security-related scenarios, ensuring that edge cases and error conditions do not result in data leakage or privilege escalation.

Role-based access control within CI systems is often overlooked but is essential for enforcing least privilege. Developers, security analysts, and operations engineers should have access to only the pipeline functions necessary for their roles. Misconfigured access can lead to unauthorized changes, privilege escalation, or tampering with the CI process itself. Logs of pipeline runs, changes to configurations, and access events should be retained and monitored for unusual activity.

Monitoring and reporting tools integrated into CI pipelines provide visibility into the effectiveness of DevSecOps efforts. Dashboards can track metrics such as vulnerability trends, time to resolution, compliance with coding standards, and the number of blocked builds due to security issues. These metrics help teams identify recurring problems, measure progress, and make data-driven decisions about where to invest in training or tooling. They also demonstrate to stakeholders that security is not an afterthought but a continuous, measurable practice embedded into daily work.

The cultural aspect of DevSecOps within CI should not be underestimated. Developers must view security not as an external barrier but as a shared responsibility. When security tools are well-integrated, fast, and provide useful feedback, developers are more likely to engage with them positively. Security teams must collaborate closely with development teams, providing clear guidelines, responsive support, and ongoing education. This collaboration builds trust and creates an environment where security is naturally embedded into the development culture.

DevSecOps in Continuous Integration represents a shift toward secure, agile, and efficient software development. It ensures that security is no longer confined to the end of the process but is present from the very first line of code. By automating security checks, managing risk proactively, and promoting a culture of collaboration, teams can deliver software that is both innovative and secure. Continuous Integration becomes not just a tool for fast delivery but a foundation for building trust in every release.

DevSecOps in Continuous Delivery

DevSecOps in Continuous Delivery represents the seamless integration of security into the final stages of the software delivery pipeline, ensuring that applications moving from staging to production meet the highest standards of security, compliance, and operational readiness. Continuous Delivery, or CD, extends the principles of Continuous Integration by enabling the automated release of validated code into production-like environments. This process allows organizations to deploy changes rapidly, frequently, and with minimal manual intervention. However, the speed and automation that make Continuous Delivery so powerful can also introduce risks if not managed carefully. Without built-in security controls, vulnerabilities and misconfigurations can be deployed just as quickly as features, exposing systems to threats. DevSecOps ensures that security is not a bottleneck but an automated, embedded, and enforceable component of delivery pipelines.

One of the foundational aspects of DevSecOps in Continuous Delivery is the use of automated gating mechanisms that evaluate the security posture of code, configurations, and infrastructure before allowing deployments to proceed. These gates act as enforcement points that validate compliance with predefined security policies. For example, before promoting an application to production, the CD pipeline might check that all critical vulnerabilities have been remediated, all dependencies are up to date, and all containers have passed security scans. If any of these criteria are not met, the deployment is halted, and actionable feedback is provided. This approach ensures that only secure artifacts reach production, and that security remains consistent and reliable across environments.

Configuration management is a key area of focus in Continuous Delivery. As applications are deployed to various environments, they are accompanied by configuration files that define runtime behavior, resource allocations, network access, logging settings, and security controls. These configurations, if mismanaged, can override secure defaults or expose systems unintentionally. DevSecOps practices ensure that configurations are treated as code, stored in version control, and validated by automated tools. Policy-as-code frameworks enforce security rules that prevent dangerous settings such as unrestricted access, disabled logging, or lack of encryption. Every deployment becomes an opportunity to validate not only the application itself but the environment in which it runs.

Another critical component of DevSecOps in Continuous Delivery is secret management. Secrets such as API keys, passwords, tokens, and certificates must be injected securely into the runtime environment. Hardcoding these values or passing them in plain text can lead to catastrophic breaches. Secure CD pipelines retrieve secrets from vaults or secret managers at deployment time, using temporary credentials and encrypted channels. Access to these secrets is restricted, monitored, and audited. Furthermore, secrets are rotated automatically to reduce exposure time in case of leaks. Integrating secret management into the delivery process ensures that security remains intact even during dynamic, automated operations.

Deployment validation is another area where DevSecOps enhances Continuous Delivery. After deployment, the system must be verified to ensure it behaves as expected and that security protections are functioning properly. Automated smoke tests, health checks, and security probes are executed immediately following deployment. These tests verify that authentication mechanisms are working, that sensitive data is encrypted, and that no new vulnerabilities have been introduced. Security monitoring tools can also assess the application's runtime behavior to detect anomalies or signs of compromise. If any issues are found, rollback mechanisms are triggered automatically, reverting the system to a known good state.

The role of observability in DevSecOps becomes even more significant in Continuous Delivery. As changes are deployed frequently, visibility into system health, performance, and security is critical. Centralized logging, metrics collection, and tracing systems capture real-time data from the application and infrastructure. Security-related events, such as access attempts, permission changes, or configuration drift, are monitored continuously. This information feeds into Security Information and Event Management platforms, enabling rapid detection and response. Alerts are configured to notify teams of suspicious activity, ensuring that deployments do not introduce silent failures or unnoticed exposures.

Continuous Delivery also requires strong governance to ensure that compliance requirements are met. Regulations such as GDPR, HIPAA, and PCI-DSS impose strict controls over data handling, access, and system behavior. DevSecOps addresses these requirements by embedding compliance checks into the delivery pipeline. Policies can be codified to ensure that data is stored securely, that only authorized roles can perform deployments, and that audit trails are maintained. These checks are automatically enforced, reducing the burden of manual audits and providing continuous assurance that the system remains within regulatory bounds.

DevSecOps in Continuous Delivery also brings attention to the importance of change control and deployment authorization. While automation reduces human error and increases speed, it must also include safeguards to prevent unauthorized or risky changes. Deployment pipelines often include approval gates where designated reviewers must validate a release before it moves to production. These reviewers consider both functional and security aspects, ensuring that the release meets business and technical requirements. Role-based access controls limit who can approve and initiate deployments, and all actions are logged for accountability.

The feedback loop is a central concept in DevSecOps and is particularly powerful in Continuous Delivery. Each deployment provides new data about system behavior, user interactions, and security posture. This data informs future development, helps refine security policies, and drives continuous improvement. Post-deployment reviews examine not only whether the feature works but whether it was deployed securely, whether it introduced any incidents, and how the system performed under load. Lessons learned are shared with development and security teams, creating a culture of transparency and resilience.

Ultimately, DevSecOps in Continuous Delivery transforms the release process into a security-enforcing engine that balances speed with control. Security is no longer something that is checked at the finish line. Instead, it is built into every stage, enforced automatically, and validated continuously. Teams can release software frequently without sacrificing safety, and organizations can respond to change with confidence. By integrating security into Continuous Delivery, DevSecOps ensures that innovation and protection move forward together, enabling the delivery of secure, stable, and high-quality applications in an increasingly complex digital world.

Role of QA in DevSecOps

The role of Quality Assurance, or QA, in DevSecOps is undergoing a fundamental transformation as software development methodologies evolve to prioritize speed, automation, and security. Traditionally, QA was primarily responsible for validating that software worked as intended and met functional requirements. This role was often isolated, positioned toward the end of the development cycle, and focused largely on finding bugs before release. However, in a DevSecOps environment, where development, operations, and security teams collaborate closely and where software is released continuously, QA must adopt a broader and more integrated approach. QA professionals are no longer just testers. They are now contributors to the stability, security, and reliability of software from the earliest stages of development through production.

In DevSecOps, the QA team plays a proactive role in embedding security and quality into the development lifecycle. This begins with their involvement during the planning and design phases of a project. Rather than waiting for features to be implemented before engaging, QA collaborates with developers, product owners, and security teams to define acceptance criteria that include not only functional correctness but also performance, usability, and security requirements. By helping shape user stories and defining test cases early, QA ensures that potential issues are addressed from the start, reducing the likelihood of flaws being introduced and making it easier to implement effective security controls.

Automation is a cornerstone of DevSecOps, and QA plays a vital role in designing and maintaining automated test suites that validate software with every code change. These test suites go beyond functional testing to include security-related tests such as input validation, authorization checks, and API security validations. Automated regression tests ensure that new features do not introduce unintended side effects or vulnerabilities. As part of the continuous integration and continuous delivery pipeline, these tests act as a quality and security gateway, preventing flawed code from progressing to production. QA engineers collaborate with developers to create these tests, ensuring they are comprehensive, reliable, and aligned with evolving business needs.

Security testing has traditionally been the domain of specialized security teams, but in DevSecOps, QA is increasingly involved in security validation activities. While they may not replace the expertise of security professionals, QA engineers can be trained to perform basic security checks, identify common vulnerabilities, and understand the security implications of different design decisions. Tools for static and dynamic analysis can be integrated into the testing workflow, and QA can be responsible for reviewing the output, verifying issues, and coordinating with developers and security specialists to address them. This collaborative approach ensures that security is not siloed but becomes part of the broader quality assurance effort.

One of the most significant contributions QA makes in a DevSecOps context is in building a culture of quality and security awareness across teams. Because QA professionals are inherently focused on risk, edge cases, and system behavior under unusual conditions, they bring a mindset that is essential for identifying weaknesses. This mindset complements the developer's focus on feature delivery and the operator's focus on stability and performance. By raising questions about how systems handle failures, how they respond to unexpected inputs, or how users might interact in unintended ways, QA fosters a culture where potential vulnerabilities and quality issues are surfaced early and addressed proactively.

In addition to automated testing, QA plays a critical role in exploratory and usability testing. Automated tools are effective for known patterns and repeatable tasks, but they may not catch subtle usability flaws or business logic vulnerabilities. QA engineers use their domain knowledge, experience, and intuition to explore the application, simulate real-world user behavior, and uncover issues that automated scripts might miss. This manual testing effort complements the automated safety net and provides deeper insight into how the application behaves in production-like conditions. In DevSecOps, where user experience and customer trust are as important as raw functionality, this human-centered testing is essential.

Monitoring and feedback loops are vital in DevSecOps, and QA teams are well-positioned to interpret and act on production data. When applications are deployed to staging or production, QA can analyze logs, performance metrics, and error reports to identify patterns that suggest emerging issues. They can use this data to refine test cases, improve automation, and inform future development cycles. Rather than ending their involvement at deployment, QA professionals continue to contribute by validating hotfixes, verifying rollback procedures, and ensuring that fixes are thoroughly tested before redeployment. This post-deployment validation closes the loop between development and operations and reinforces continuous improvement.

Collaboration is at the heart of DevSecOps, and QA is uniquely situated to bridge the gaps between teams. They understand both technical implementation details and user expectations, making them effective communicators between developers, product owners, security engineers, and system administrators. By facilitating discussions about risk, reliability, and user impact, QA helps align priorities and ensure that everyone is working toward shared goals. In environments where DevSecOps is still maturing, QA can lead initiatives to integrate testing and security tools into pipelines, define quality metrics, and establish test-driven development practices that drive better outcomes.

The tools QA uses in a DevSecOps setting are also evolving. In addition to traditional test automation frameworks, QA teams now leverage containerized test environments, service virtualization, and continuous testing platforms that allow for faster feedback and more realistic test conditions. Security scanners, code quality analyzers, and performance testing tools are part of the QA toolkit, and the results from these tools feed into dashboards and reports that inform stakeholders in real time. QA engineers must be skilled not only in scripting and test case design but also in interpreting tool output, configuring integrations, and managing test environments that reflect the complexity of modern systems.

In this new era, QA is no longer a separate phase or a final checkpoint. It is an integral and continuous part of the development and delivery lifecycle. The QA team evolves from being gatekeepers to enablers of secure, high-quality software. They drive the adoption of best practices, maintain the balance between speed and reliability, and ensure that security is not compromised in the pursuit of agility. The role of QA in DevSecOps is to advocate for the user, validate the system, and challenge assumptions in ways that lead to more resilient, secure, and trustworthy applications. This elevated role demands new skills, new tools, and a mindset that embraces collaboration, innovation, and accountability at every stage of software creation.

Incident Response and Recovery Planning

Incident response and recovery planning are critical components of any mature DevSecOps strategy. As organizations adopt faster, automated, and cloud-native development models, the attack surface expands and the pace of change increases. While prevention and detection mechanisms are essential, they cannot guarantee complete protection. Security incidents are inevitable, whether caused by human error, software vulnerabilities, insider threats, or sophisticated external attacks. The key to minimizing damage, maintaining trust, and restoring operations lies in having a well-defined, rehearsed, and integrated incident response and recovery plan that operates effectively in high-pressure situations.

In a DevSecOps environment, incident response is not the sole responsibility of a separate security team. Instead, it is a shared responsibility involving developers, operations, security professionals, and often stakeholders from legal, communications, and executive leadership. This multidisciplinary collaboration ensures that the organization can respond to incidents holistically, considering both technical remediation and business continuity. From the moment an incident is suspected, time becomes a critical factor. A delay in response can result in increased data loss, system outages, reputational harm, or regulatory penalties. Having predefined roles, communication protocols, and response procedures enables teams to act decisively and effectively under pressure.

The first phase of any incident response plan is preparation. In this stage, organizations define their incident response policies, form response teams, and establish tools and processes for managing incidents. This includes setting up secure communication channels, logging and monitoring systems, and access to forensic tools. A critical aspect of preparation is defining what constitutes a security incident. Not every anomaly or failed login attempt rises to the level of a full-scale incident. Categorizing incidents based on severity and impact helps teams prioritize their efforts and allocate resources appropriately. Preparation also involves training and regular simulation exercises, often called tabletop scenarios, where teams practice responding to hypothetical incidents to refine their coordination and decision-making skills.

Detection and identification form the next phase of incident response. In a DevSecOps setting, this relies heavily on continuous monitoring and observability. Logs from applications, servers, containers, and network devices must be aggregated and analyzed in real time to detect suspicious behavior. Anomalies such as sudden spikes in network traffic, unexpected configuration changes, or failed authentication attempts can serve as early indicators of compromise. Security Information and Event Management systems play a crucial role in correlating data from multiple sources and generating alerts for investigation. At this stage, rapid and accurate identification of the incident is essential. Teams must determine what systems are affected, how the breach occurred, and whether the threat is ongoing.

Once an incident is confirmed, the focus shifts to containment. The goal of containment is to limit the spread and impact of the incident while preserving evidence for investigation. In a cloud-native environment, this might involve isolating compromised containers, revoking access tokens, or disabling vulnerable services. Containment strategies must balance speed with precision. Overreacting by shutting down systems indiscriminately can cause unnecessary disruption, while underreacting can allow the attacker to continue their activity. Well-defined containment playbooks provide guidance on actions to take based on incident type and severity. These playbooks are developed in advance and tailored to the organization's architecture and risk profile.

Eradication follows containment and involves removing the root cause of the incident. This step may include patching vulnerabilities, deleting malware, resetting credentials, and hardening configurations. In DevSecOps environments, eradication is often supported by automation. Infrastructure as Code can be used to rebuild compromised systems from clean templates, ensuring consistency and eliminating manual errors. Automated deployment pipelines allow teams to apply fixes quickly and confidently across environments. Collaboration with development teams is critical during eradication, especially when the cause of the incident is related to application logic or third-party dependencies. The goal is not just to remove the threat but to ensure it cannot reoccur.

Recovery is the process of restoring normal operations after the threat has been eliminated. In modern systems, this includes restarting services, validating data integrity, reapplying security controls, and gradually reintroducing affected systems to the network. Recovery plans must account for dependencies between services and the need to test thoroughly before returning to full operation. Clear communication with stakeholders, including customers and partners, is essential during this phase. Transparent updates about service availability, data impact, and steps taken to resolve the issue help maintain trust and manage reputational risk. Recovery timelines and priorities should be defined in advance and regularly reviewed based on business impact.

Post-incident analysis is a crucial phase that is often neglected. Once the immediate crisis is resolved, the organization must conduct a thorough review of the incident. This includes a timeline of events, an analysis of root causes, the effectiveness of the response, and identification of gaps in detection, containment, or recovery. These lessons learned are then used to improve tools, processes, and training. Post-incident reviews should be documented and shared with relevant stakeholders, and they should lead to actionable follow-ups. This retrospective approach turns each incident into an opportunity for growth and increased resilience.

Incident response planning must also integrate with regulatory and legal requirements. Depending on the nature of the incident and the jurisdiction, organizations may be required to report breaches to authorities, notify affected users, or follow specific protocols. Legal teams must be involved early in the process to guide compliance efforts and manage potential liabilities. Communication teams also play a role, crafting messages for internal and external audiences to ensure consistency, accuracy, and timeliness. Coordinating these non-technical aspects is just as important as managing the technical response.

Incorporating incident response and recovery into DevSecOps requires a cultural shift as well. It means accepting that incidents will happen and designing systems to be resilient, not just secure. Teams must adopt a blameless mindset, focusing on systemic improvements rather than individual fault. It also means investing in tools and processes that enable rapid detection, collaboration, and automation. Continuous improvement, a core DevOps principle, applies to security as well. By treating incident response as an iterative process, organizations build confidence in their ability to adapt and respond to future threats.

Incident response and recovery are no longer isolated functions. They are integrated into the daily operations of development and operations teams. In the world of DevSecOps, where code is deployed frequently and environments change constantly, the ability to detect, contain, and recover from incidents rapidly is a defining capability. It protects not only systems and data but also user trust, business continuity, and the reputation of the organization. A well-executed response plan is a demonstration of preparedness, resilience, and a commitment to security in the face of an ever-evolving threat landscape.

Monitoring and Logging for Security

Monitoring and logging for security are indispensable practices in any DevSecOps strategy, providing the visibility, traceability, and intelligence required to detect, investigate, and respond to threats in real time. As organizations embrace automation, containerization, and cloud-native architectures, the complexity of their systems increases exponentially. This complexity brings flexibility and scalability, but it also introduces more entry points, interconnected services, and potential blind spots. Without robust monitoring and logging, teams are effectively operating in the dark, unaware of malicious activity, policy violations, misconfigurations, or internal misuse. In contrast, when done correctly, security monitoring and logging become the eyes and ears of the entire infrastructure, offering early warnings and actionable insights that can prevent small issues from escalating into major incidents.

Monitoring for security begins with understanding the scope and surface area of what needs to be observed. Every system component, from the application code and underlying infrastructure to user activity and network traffic, generates data that can reveal the system's current state. Monitoring involves collecting, aggregating, and analyzing this data to identify anomalies and patterns that may indicate malicious behavior. Effective security monitoring includes metrics such as failed login attempts, unauthorized access to sensitive resources, unexpected configuration changes, lateral movement across systems, unusual network activity, and execution of suspicious processes. The earlier and more accurately these events are detected, the faster a response can be initiated to contain and mitigate potential damage.

Logging is the foundational layer that enables effective monitoring. Logs provide a structured, chronological record of system activity and behavior. They capture events such as API calls, user authentication, file access, database queries, and application errors. In a DevSecOps environment, logs are generated from a wide range of sources, including web servers, application runtimes, load balancers, containers, cloud services, CI/CD pipelines, and third-party tools. The sheer volume of logs can be overwhelming, so proper log management is essential. Logs must be centralized, normalized, and indexed to make them searchable and usable. Centralized logging platforms, such as Elasticsearch, Splunk, or cloud-native solutions like AWS CloudWatch and Azure Monitor, allow security teams to correlate events across distributed environments and detect patterns that might otherwise be missed.

One of the key principles in logging for security is to log with purpose. Not all logs are equally valuable, and indiscriminate logging can consume resources without delivering insight. Teams must determine which events are critical for security, how much detail should be captured, and how long logs should be retained. For example, logging every request to a public web page may not be useful, but logging failed authentication attempts or access to sensitive configuration files is crucial. Security logs should include context such as timestamps, user identifiers, IP addresses, session IDs, and request parameters to support forensic analysis and traceability. This context allows teams to reconstruct events, understand the attack path, and assess the scope of an incident.

To be effective, monitoring and logging systems must be integrated into the development and deployment lifecycle. Logging should be considered a nonfunctional requirement and included in application design. Developers must be trained to instrument code properly, using structured logging formats and consistent log levels to differentiate between information, warnings, and errors. Logging frameworks should support dynamic configuration to allow for increased verbosity during debugging or incidents without redeploying applications. Logs should never contain sensitive data such as passwords, tokens, or personally identifiable information in plaintext. Proper redaction, anonymization, or encryption mechanisms must be in place to protect log integrity and prevent data leakage.

Real-time monitoring tools complement logging by providing dashboards, alerts, and automated responses based on predefined thresholds or behavioral analysis. These tools use log data, performance metrics, and telemetry signals to generate insights and trigger notifications when suspicious activity is detected. Security Information and Event Management systems aggregate and analyze this data to produce meaningful alerts. Advanced SIEMs incorporate machine learning and threat intelligence to detect subtle anomalies and correlate them with known attack signatures or tactics. When integrated into the DevSecOps pipeline, these systems enable continuous monitoring and help enforce security policies dynamically across all environments.

In cloud-native and microservices environments, monitoring becomes more challenging due to the ephemeral nature of containers, serverless functions, and dynamic scaling. Traditional logging methods may not capture short-lived events or correlate logs across transient services. To address this, distributed tracing and observability platforms are employed to track requests as they flow through multiple components. These traces provide a complete picture of how a transaction is processed, where delays or failures occur, and whether any component behaves abnormally. Combining logs, metrics, and traces provides a comprehensive observability stack that enhances visibility into system behavior and security posture.

Access control and integrity of log data are equally important. Logs must be protected from tampering, deletion, or unauthorized access. Logging systems should enforce role-based access controls, encryption at rest and in transit, and immutable storage options where necessary. Audit trails must be preserved to satisfy regulatory requirements and support post-incident investigations. Retention policies should align with legal and business needs, balancing the cost of storage with the value of long-term visibility. Logs that are too short-lived may hinder investigations, while retaining excessive logs without purpose can lead to unnecessary risk and cost.

Monitoring and logging also play a vital role in compliance and governance. Regulations such as GDPR, HIPAA, PCI-DSS, and ISO standards require organizations to maintain records of system activity, access to sensitive data, and evidence of security controls. Automated compliance dashboards, powered by log data, provide real-time visibility into whether systems are operating within defined policies. They also enable organizations to generate audit reports quickly and respond to regulatory inquiries with confidence. In this way, monitoring and logging become both a technical and strategic asset.

The culture around monitoring and logging must evolve alongside the technology. In a DevSecOps environment, these practices are not the responsibility of a single team but are shared across developers, operations, and security. Developers must build observability into their applications, operations teams must maintain the infrastructure for data collection and analysis, and security teams must define detection rules and incident workflows. This collaboration ensures that monitoring and logging serve the broader goals of resilience, security, and continuous improvement.

As threats grow more advanced and systems more complex, monitoring and logging provide the foundational visibility required to maintain control. They transform raw events into actionable insights, enabling rapid detection of threats, efficient response to incidents, and informed decisions about future improvements. When implemented with purpose and precision, monitoring and logging for security become not just a technical necessity but a force multiplier for the entire DevSecOps lifecycle.

Integrating SIEM with DevSecOps

Integrating a Security Information and Event Management system, or SIEM, into a DevSecOps framework is essential for creating a robust and responsive security posture. As software development cycles accelerate and cloud-native architectures become the norm, security must evolve to keep pace. DevSecOps seeks to embed security into every phase of the software delivery lifecycle, making it a shared responsibility across development, operations, and security teams. A SIEM provides the visibility, correlation, and real-time analysis required to detect, investigate, and respond to security events within this high-velocity environment. Rather than functioning as an isolated tool used solely by security analysts, a modern SIEM, when integrated properly, becomes a foundational element of the entire DevSecOps pipeline.

SIEM systems operate by collecting and aggregating logs and event data from a wide range of sources. These sources include application logs, operating systems, cloud platforms, containers, endpoints, authentication systems, and network devices. In a DevSecOps context, this data must also come from development tools, CI/CD pipelines, infrastructure as code templates, and container orchestration platforms. The power of a SIEM lies in its ability to normalize this disparate data, correlate it in real time, and surface patterns that indicate malicious activity or policy violations. By centralizing this visibility, the SIEM becomes a critical mechanism for maintaining situational awareness across a constantly evolving environment.

The integration process begins with identifying the sources that are most relevant to the DevSecOps lifecycle. Version control systems, for instance, can provide valuable insight into who is making code changes, when, and how often. This information can be correlated with build and deployment activities from CI/CD systems to detect anomalies, such as unexpected code commits or unauthorized deployment attempts. Similarly, infrastructure as code templates stored in repositories like Terraform or CloudFormation must be monitored for unauthorized modifications. These templates often control critical resources such as firewalls, access permissions, and network configurations. Unauthorized or unreviewed changes can open the door to serious vulnerabilities. SIEM systems can be configured to alert on such changes, enabling immediate investigation and rollback if necessary.

Once relevant data sources are connected, the next step involves developing rules and use cases tailored to the DevSecOps environment. These rules define what types of behavior are considered suspicious or indicative of compromise. For example, if a developer account suddenly initiates a high volume of changes across multiple repositories or makes changes during unusual hours, the SIEM can generate an alert. If a pipeline executes a deployment from an untrusted source or pushes an image that has not passed security scans, that behavior can be flagged for review. These detection rules must be designed to align with the organization's risk appetite, compliance obligations, and operational realities. Collaboration between security engineers, DevOps specialists, and developers is necessary to fine-tune these rules and avoid both false positives and blind spots.

Automation is a key aspect of SIEM integration within DevSecOps. The goal is to reduce mean time to detection and response without slowing down the delivery process. When a SIEM detects a potential incident, it can trigger automated workflows to contain or mitigate the threat. These actions might include revoking access tokens, quarantining containers, scaling down compromised services, or initiating a rollback to a known good state. Integration with Security Orchestration,

Automation, and Response (SOAR) platforms enhances this capability further, enabling complex incident response playbooks to execute with minimal human intervention. This automation allows organizations to maintain agility while preserving a strong security posture.

Contextual awareness is another advantage of SIEM integration. Because SIEM systems ingest and correlate data from so many sources, they can provide a full narrative of how an attack or incident unfolded. For example, a SIEM might detect that a misconfigured IAM policy was introduced via a pull request, which led to unauthorized access, followed by data exfiltration through an unmonitored API. Understanding the chain of events is essential for effective incident response, root cause analysis, and long-term remediation. In the DevSecOps model, where incidents must be addressed quickly to maintain velocity and reliability, having access to this comprehensive context reduces time spent on investigation and improves decision-making.

Visibility into compliance is another benefit of integrating SIEM with DevSecOps. Regulatory frameworks such as GDPR, HIPAA, and PCI-DSS require organizations to log access to sensitive data, monitor system activity, and retain evidence of security controls. SIEMs can provide real-time dashboards, audit reports, and historical queries that demonstrate compliance across development, staging, and production environments. This not only reduces the burden of audit preparation but also ensures that compliance is continuous rather than event-driven. By embedding compliance monitoring into the development lifecycle, organizations reduce the risk of violations and improve accountability.

A well-integrated SIEM also enhances security culture. Developers and DevOps engineers begin to see security not as an afterthought or obstacle but as a core aspect of their daily work. Alerts generated by the SIEM can be routed into chat systems, issue trackers, or notification platforms used by development teams. When developers are notified immediately about risky behavior in their code, pipeline, or infrastructure configurations, they can respond quickly and learn from the experience. This feedback loop reinforces secure habits and encourages proactive risk management. Over time, this cultural shift leads to greater collaboration, shared responsibility, and continuous improvement.

Scalability and performance are important considerations when integrating SIEM into fast-moving DevSecOps pipelines. The volume of logs and events generated by automated deployments, microservices, containers, and dynamic infrastructure can be massive. SIEM solutions must be configured to scale horizontally, ingest data efficiently, and prioritize high-value alerts. Filtering, aggregation, and intelligent indexing are essential to ensure that the system remains responsive and usable. Additionally, the retention of data must be managed according to business needs, balancing the value of long-term storage with cost and performance concerns.

Finally, continuous refinement is necessary for a successful SIEM integration. As the environment changes, new services are added, and new threats emerge, detection rules, dashboards, and playbooks must be updated. Periodic reviews, threat modeling exercises, and incident retrospectives help ensure that the SIEM remains aligned with current risks and operational goals. This adaptability reflects the DevSecOps philosophy itself: a commitment to learning, iteration, and resilience.

Integrating a SIEM with DevSecOps is not just about adding a tool. It is about creating a system of awareness, accountability, and agility that spans the entire software lifecycle. By bridging the gap between security and operations, SIEM integration empowers teams to detect threats faster, respond more effectively, and build software with greater confidence. As organizations continue to push the boundaries of digital transformation, a properly integrated SIEM becomes not only a source of protection but also a driver of innovation and trust.

Vulnerability Management Automation

Vulnerability management automation is an essential practice in modern DevSecOps environments, enabling organizations to identify, assess, prioritize, and remediate security weaknesses at the speed and scale required by continuous development and deployment. As applications grow more complex and the number of software components and third-party dependencies increases, manual methods of vulnerability detection and tracking become insufficient. Automation brings consistency, speed, and reliability to a process that is often overwhelmed by the volume of vulnerabilities discovered on a daily basis. Without automation, vulnerabilities can remain unaddressed for extended periods, increasing the likelihood of exploitation and data breaches. Automating vulnerability management allows security teams to keep pace with development, reduce risk exposure, and maintain compliance without becoming a bottleneck to delivery.

The process begins with continuous scanning across the entire technology stack. Vulnerability scanners must be integrated into all relevant stages of the software development lifecycle. Static application security testing tools analyze source code for coding flaws and insecure patterns. Software composition analysis tools inspect open-source dependencies for known vulnerabilities. Container scanning tools review container images for outdated packages and misconfigurations. Infrastructure as code scanning tools assess deployment templates for insecure configurations. These scans are triggered automatically during the build phase in CI pipelines, ensuring that issues are identified as soon as they are introduced into the codebase or dependency tree. This early detection reduces the cost and effort of remediation while ensuring that vulnerable artifacts never make it into production.

Automated vulnerability detection must be paired with effective prioritization. Not all vulnerabilities pose the same level of risk. Severity scores such as CVSS provide a baseline for understanding the technical impact, but context is equally important. A critical vulnerability in a package that is not used at runtime, or that is protected behind multiple layers of security controls, may not represent an immediate threat. Conversely, a medium-severity vulnerability in a public-facing authentication module could be a significant risk. Automation tools can apply contextual analysis to identify which vulnerabilities are truly exploitable based on usage, exposure, asset importance, and available mitigations. By correlating vulnerability data with asset inventories, business impact, and threat intelligence feeds, organizations can create a prioritized list of issues that require action.

Once vulnerabilities are identified and prioritized, the next step is automated remediation and response. This includes capabilities such as automated patching, dependency upgrades, or code refactoring suggestions. Integration with version control systems allows tools to generate pull requests or merge requests that update affected libraries or adjust configurations. These suggested changes can be reviewed and tested by development teams as part of their normal workflow, reducing friction and increasing the likelihood of timely remediation. For containers and infrastructure, new images or templates can be automatically rebuilt with secure components and pushed through the deployment pipeline. This approach not only shortens the time to resolution but also reduces reliance on manual intervention, which can be error-prone and inconsistent.

In large organizations with thousands of assets, centralization of vulnerability data is key to making automation work at scale. A vulnerability management platform aggregates findings from various tools, tracks remediation status, and provides dashboards for security, development, and compliance teams. These platforms offer visibility into vulnerability trends, exposure levels, and team performance. Integration with ticketing systems ensures that vulnerabilities are converted into actionable tasks assigned to the right teams. Service level objectives can be defined based on vulnerability severity, and automation ensures that escalations are triggered when deadlines are not met. This closed-loop process enforces accountability while reducing the overhead of manual tracking and coordination.

Automation also plays a significant role in measuring and reporting on risk and compliance. Regulatory frameworks such as PCI-DSS, HIPAA, and SOC 2 require organizations to demonstrate that they are managing vulnerabilities in a timely and effective manner. Automated tools generate reports that show scan coverage, remediation timelines, and risk trends. These reports can be scheduled, customized, and delivered to stakeholders without additional manual effort. Compliance audits become more streamlined when data is consistently collected, centralized, and presented in a format that aligns with auditor expectations. This visibility supports proactive governance and reduces the chance of compliance violations due to overlooked vulnerabilities.

Another benefit of automation is the ability to implement dynamic risk mitigation when immediate remediation is not possible. Sometimes patches or upgrades are delayed due to business constraints, testing requirements, or application compatibility issues. In such cases, security controls such as virtual patching, web application firewalls, or runtime protection can be automatically configured to block exploitation attempts. These compensating controls serve as a temporary shield while permanent fixes are prepared. Automation ensures that these controls are applied consistently, monitored for effectiveness, and removed once remediation is complete.

Security awareness and collaboration are also enhanced through automation. Developers receive immediate feedback when vulnerabilities are introduced, along with actionable guidance on how to resolve them. This reinforces secure coding practices and accelerates learning. Dashboards and notifications keep stakeholders informed about the current state of vulnerability management, fostering a shared understanding of risk and progress. When teams can see how their efforts contribute to improved security outcomes, they become more engaged in the process. Automation provides the structure and transparency needed to sustain this collaborative culture.

Despite its many advantages, automated vulnerability management must be approached thoughtfully to avoid pitfalls. False positives, tool sprawl, and alert fatigue can reduce the effectiveness of automation if not managed carefully. Tools must be selected and configured to balance thoroughness with accuracy. Policies must define which vulnerabilities should block a release and which can be addressed over time. Exceptions must be documented and reviewed regularly. Human oversight remains essential to validate findings, resolve ambiguity, and make context-driven decisions. Automation enhances the process, but it does not replace the need for skilled professionals who understand the nuances of security and software development.

The continuous nature of DevSecOps makes automation not only beneficial but necessary. With every code commit, pipeline run, and deployment, there is potential for new vulnerabilities to be introduced. Manual processes cannot keep up with this pace. Automated vulnerability management provides the scalability, consistency, and speed required to protect modern applications without slowing down innovation. It transforms vulnerability response from a reactive firefight into a proactive and controlled discipline. As threat landscapes evolve and development cycles accelerate, organizations that embrace automation in vulnerability management will be better positioned to reduce risk, maintain trust, and deliver secure software with confidence.

Managing Third-Party Risks

Managing third-party risks has become a critical component of cybersecurity strategy within modern DevSecOps practices. As organizations increasingly rely on external vendors, libraries, frameworks, APIs, cloud services, and software-as-a-service platforms to build and run their applications, the attack surface expands beyond internal control. Every third-party integration introduces a potential entry point for attackers, and history has shown that adversaries often exploit the weakest link in the supply chain rather than targeting heavily fortified systems directly. Managing these risks effectively requires a combination of process, technology, continuous monitoring, and collaboration across security, development, and procurement teams.

The first step in managing third-party risks is gaining visibility into what third-party components are in use. This includes both direct dependencies explicitly used in codebases and transitive dependencies brought in indirectly through packages and plugins. Modern software development often involves assembling rather than writing code from scratch, with projects leveraging thousands of open-source components. Without clear visibility, organizations cannot assess the risk profile or stay informed about vulnerabilities. A comprehensive software bill of materials is essential for tracking these components. Automated tools can analyze repositories, containers, and configuration files to generate real-time inventories, ensuring that security teams know exactly what is running in production and where each component originated.

Once visibility is established, the next challenge is assessing the security posture of each third-party element. Not all dependencies are created equal. Some are maintained by active communities, receive regular updates, and follow responsible disclosure practices. Others may be outdated, abandoned, or maintained by a single individual. Security teams must evaluate each component's history of vulnerabilities, the responsiveness of maintainers, the presence of security documentation, and adherence to secure development practices. These evaluations help determine which third parties can be trusted and which should be avoided, replaced, or monitored more closely. This assessment extends to vendors and service providers as well. Before integrating a third-party SaaS product or cloud service, organizations must review its security certifications, data protection policies, breach history, and compliance with industry standards.

Automated risk scoring can assist in prioritizing which third-party risks require immediate attention. Tools that integrate with threat intelligence feeds and vulnerability databases can correlate known issues with components used within the organization's environments. When a new vulnerability is disclosed, these tools can automatically determine which applications are affected and generate alerts for remediation. Risk scoring considers both the severity of the vulnerability and the exposure level based on usage context. This enables teams to focus resources on the most critical threats rather than being overwhelmed by the volume of less impactful issues. Integration of these tools into the CI/CD pipeline ensures that risk assessments are performed continuously and that new code cannot introduce insecure dependencies undetected.

Managing third-party risks also involves defining and enforcing policies for third-party usage. Development teams should follow guidelines that dictate which sources are approved for pulling dependencies, what licensing terms are acceptable, and how new packages are introduced into the environment. Gatekeeping mechanisms can be implemented in CI pipelines to block the use of unapproved or insecure components. Code review processes should include checks for new third-party additions, and developers should be trained to understand the risks associated with importing unfamiliar packages. Encouraging the use of trusted registries and verified sources reduces the likelihood of integrating malicious or compromised libraries.

Third-party risk does not end once a component is added. Continuous monitoring is necessary to detect changes in the security status of dependencies over time. A component that is safe today may become a risk tomorrow due to the discovery of a new vulnerability or a compromise in its supply chain. Attackers have increasingly targeted open-source software by injecting malicious code into widely used packages, sometimes by taking control of a maintainer's account or compromising the distribution channel. Organizations must monitor for such incidents and have processes in place to respond rapidly. This includes validating checksums of downloaded packages, using signed artifacts where available, and restricting egress traffic to prevent unauthorized downloads during build processes.

Incident response plans should include specific procedures for third-party compromise scenarios. When a vulnerability is disclosed in a widely used library or a third-party vendor suffers a breach, organizations must be able to quickly determine their exposure, assess potential impact, and initiate mitigation steps. This might involve upgrading to a patched version, isolating affected systems, revoking credentials, or applying temporary compensating controls. Communication with vendors and maintainers is key during these incidents. Security teams must establish channels for receiving updates and advisories and should actively participate in communities where critical updates are shared.

Legal and contractual measures also play an important role in managing third-party risks. Vendor agreements should include security requirements, data handling obligations, and breach notification clauses. Service-level agreements must define acceptable downtime, recovery objectives, and responsibilities in the event of a security incident. Where possible, organizations should require vendors to undergo regular security assessments and provide audit reports. For cloud-based services, shared responsibility models must be clearly understood, with both parties aware of who is responsible for securing specific components of the stack.

Cultural alignment is another dimension of third-party risk. Security is not just a technical consideration but also a reflection of values, practices, and accountability. Organizations should prefer vendors and maintainers who demonstrate a commitment to secure development, transparent communication, and responsible vulnerability disclosure. Working with partners who share a security-first mindset strengthens the overall ecosystem and reduces the likelihood of misaligned priorities leading to unaddressed risks.

Ultimately, managing third-party risks in a DevSecOps world requires integrating security at every level where external code, services, or vendors intersect with the development process. It requires proactive identification of components, continuous evaluation of their security posture, enforcement of usage policies, and rapid response when issues arise. Automation and tooling help scale these practices, while governance and collaboration ensure that security remains a shared priority. As dependency chains grow longer and software ecosystems become more interconnected, organizations that take a structured and vigilant approach to third-party risk management will be better equipped to maintain trust, resilience, and security across their software supply chains.

Governance and Policy as Code

Governance and policy as code have become foundational elements in the modern DevSecOps approach, addressing the need for consistency, transparency, and enforceability across complex, fast-moving development environments. As organizations scale their software delivery processes, traditional manual methods of enforcing compliance and governance are no longer sufficient. They are too slow, error-prone, and disconnected from the automated workflows that power continuous integration and deployment. Policy as code offers a powerful solution by embedding governance directly into the development and operational pipelines. It transforms static rules and spreadsheets into machine-readable logic that can be enforced automatically, allowing teams to innovate quickly while ensuring alignment with internal controls, industry standards, and regulatory requirements.

At its core, governance refers to the structures, processes, and practices that ensure accountability, compliance, and control within an organization. In a DevSecOps context, governance encompasses decisions around who can deploy to production, what infrastructure configurations are permitted, how sensitive data is handled, and whether changes align with business and legal obligations. These rules often originate from security policies, architectural standards, or external regulatory frameworks. Without a way to operationalize them, they risk becoming irrelevant to the rapid, automated workflows that define DevSecOps environments. Policy as code bridges this gap by allowing these rules to be expressed in a format that machines can interpret and enforce without human intervention.

Policy as code begins by codifying governance requirements using a declarative language or framework. This could include tools like Open Policy Agent, HashiCorp Sentinel, Azure Policy, or custom rule engines tailored to the organization's infrastructure. Policies might define acceptable resource configurations, such as requiring encryption on storage buckets, denying public access to virtual machines, or enforcing naming conventions for cloud resources. In the CI/CD pipeline, these policies are evaluated automatically whenever code, infrastructure definitions, or deployment configurations are committed. If a proposed change violates a policy, the pipeline fails, and actionable feedback is returned to the developer. This immediate response reinforces best practices, prevents violations from progressing further, and allows developers to fix issues early.

The power of policy as code lies in its consistency and scalability. Manual reviews and ad hoc approvals introduce variability, delay, and the risk of oversight. Automated policy enforcement ensures that every environment—whether development, staging, or production—adheres to the same standards. It eliminates the need to rely solely on documentation, checklists, or verbal communication to uphold governance. Instead, the rules are built directly into the systems that manage infrastructure and deployments. This automation does not just reduce human error; it also provides a consistent audit trail, showing exactly when and how policies were evaluated, what decisions were made, and why those decisions occurred. These logs are invaluable for compliance, incident response, and continuous improvement.

Policy as code also supports modularity and reusability. Governance frameworks can be designed using reusable policy modules that represent common controls across projects. These modules can then be composed into larger policy sets tailored to specific applications, teams, or environments. This approach promotes standardization while allowing for flexibility where needed. Teams can inherit baseline policies and override or extend them with context-specific rules. For example, a central security policy might enforce encryption across all cloud services, while a team-specific policy ensures that database credentials are pulled from a secrets manager and not hardcoded into environment variables. By managing policies as code in version control systems, organizations gain the same benefits of collaboration, peer review, and version history that apply to application code.

Governance through policy as code also enables proactive compliance. Regulatory obligations such as GDPR, HIPAA, PCI-DSS, and ISO 27001 require organizations to demonstrate that security and privacy controls are in place and operating effectively. By codifying these requirements into policy rules and integrating them into the pipeline, organizations move from periodic compliance checks to continuous validation. Every commit, every infrastructure change, and every deployment is automatically tested against the relevant policies. Violations can be flagged instantly, and changes can be blocked until compliance is restored. This reduces the risk of non-compliance and streamlines audit preparation by providing real-time evidence of control effectiveness and policy enforcement.

Another important aspect of policy as code is the empowerment of teams to self-serve while remaining within governance boundaries. In traditional models, central security or operations teams often act as gatekeepers, reviewing and approving changes manually. This slows down development and creates tension between speed and control. With policy as code, governance becomes decentralized and embedded. Development teams can move quickly and make decisions autonomously, confident that automated policies will prevent them from violating rules. This creates a culture of trust, accountability, and speed, where governance is not a hindrance but a guide that enables safe and efficient progress.

Monitoring and alerting mechanisms complement policy enforcement by providing visibility into policy violations and their frequency. Dashboards can show how many policy checks are passing or failing across teams, which controls are most often violated, and whether compliance is improving over time. These insights help security and governance leaders understand where to focus training, improve policies, or address systemic issues. For example, if a high percentage of failed deployments are due to missing encryption settings, it may indicate the need for better documentation or defaults rather than individual developer failure.

However, policy as code must be introduced carefully to avoid disrupting productivity or creating bottlenecks. Policies must be clear, actionable, and aligned with business goals. They should be tested thoroughly in lower environments before being enforced in production. Developers should be involved in policy design to ensure that rules are realistic and understandable. A policy that blocks a deployment without explaining why or offering a path to remediation can create frustration and resistance. Good policies strike a balance between strictness and flexibility, providing guardrails rather than barriers.

Training and communication are essential for successful adoption. Teams must understand the purpose of policy as code, how to interpret policy violations, and how to resolve them. Documentation, workshops, and office hours with policy authors can facilitate this understanding. As policies evolve, changes should be communicated clearly and reviewed collaboratively to maintain alignment and transparency.

Governance and policy as code are not just about preventing risk—they are about enabling innovation within a framework of trust. They align security and compliance with the realities of cloud-native development, providing automated safeguards that scale with the organization. They reduce friction between teams, eliminate ambiguity, and create a reliable foundation for secure, compliant, and agile software delivery. As DevSecOps continues to mature, the ability to encode governance into the fabric of development will be a defining capability for organizations that seek both speed and security in a digital-first world.

Penetration Testing in DevSecOps

Penetration testing in DevSecOps plays a critical role in validating the security posture of applications, infrastructure, and environments by simulating real-world attacks under controlled conditions. In traditional software development models, penetration testing often occurred near the end of the development cycle, just before release. While this approach provided a final safety check, it also introduced delays and uncovered issues at a time when fixing them was costly and disruptive. DevSecOps, with its emphasis on continuous integration, continuous delivery, and embedded security, redefines the role of penetration testing by making it more iterative, automated, and integrated into the development pipeline. The goal is to identify vulnerabilities early, address them quickly, and ensure that security assessments evolve alongside the software.

Penetration testing, or ethical hacking, involves using manual and automated techniques to exploit weaknesses in systems in the same way a malicious actor would. The tester attempts to bypass security controls, escalate privileges, access sensitive data, and demonstrate the potential impact of successful exploitation. This not only reveals technical flaws but also uncovers gaps in detection, response, and configuration. In a DevSecOps context, penetration testing helps teams move beyond checkbox compliance and surface the true security risks facing their applications and systems.

One of the challenges of integrating penetration testing into DevSecOps is reconciling the traditional cadence of pen testing with the rapid pace of development. Modern applications can be updated multiple times a day, and manual penetration tests cannot keep up with this frequency. To address this, organizations adopt a hybrid model that combines continuous automated security testing with periodic targeted manual penetration assessments. Automated tools simulate common attack vectors, test for known vulnerabilities, and validate configuration hygiene as part of the CI/CD pipeline. These tools run at every build, every pull request, or every deployment, ensuring that regressions and newly introduced flaws are caught early.

Manual penetration testing, on the other hand, is reserved for high-impact scenarios that require human creativity, intuition, and contextual understanding. These assessments focus on business logic flaws, chained vulnerabilities, zero-day exploits, and application-specific risks that automated tools cannot detect. In a DevSecOps workflow, manual pen testing is often conducted in pre-production environments or on major releases. It is planned in coordination with development and security teams and often focuses on areas identified as high risk based on threat modeling, architecture reviews, or previous findings. The results of these tests feed directly into the backlog, where vulnerabilities are triaged, prioritized, and remediated just like bugs or feature enhancements.

To be effective in DevSecOps, penetration testing must be closely aligned with agile practices. This means breaking down large testing engagements into smaller, incremental efforts that align with sprints or feature releases. Rather than waiting for a comprehensive test of the entire application, pen testers focus on new modules, updated APIs, or changes in authentication workflows. They work collaboratively with developers and product teams, often providing real-time feedback and participating in sprint planning and retrospectives. This continuous engagement shifts the perception of penetration testing from a gatekeeping function to a value-adding partner in the development process.

Another critical component of penetration testing in DevSecOps is integration with existing tools and workflows. Findings from pen tests should be documented in the same systems used by developers, such as Jira, GitHub Issues, or Azure Boards. This ensures visibility, traceability, and accountability. Vulnerabilities should include detailed descriptions, reproduction steps, risk ratings, and recommended fixes. When possible, the testing team should also provide proof-of-concept exploits or scripts that demonstrate the issue clearly. Automated findings can be exported directly into these platforms, while manual findings are often added after review and verification.

Metrics play a vital role in measuring the effectiveness of penetration testing and its integration into DevSecOps. Organizations track metrics such as the number of vulnerabilities discovered per release, the average time to remediate, the percentage of critical issues resolved within service level agreements, and the recurrence of previously closed issues. These metrics inform security posture, resource allocation, and overall maturity. By comparing results over time, teams can determine whether security is improving and identify areas where additional controls or training are needed.

Security training and awareness also benefit from penetration testing. When developers see how their code can be exploited, it reinforces secure coding practices and deepens their understanding of real-world threats. Many organizations use findings from pen tests as teaching tools during post-mortems, lunch-and-learns, or internal workshops. Red and blue team exercises, where penetration testers simulate attacks and defenders attempt to detect and respond, provide a hands-on way to improve coordination, communication, and preparedness. These exercises are particularly effective in DevSecOps environments, where cross-functional collaboration is critical.

Modern tooling continues to enhance the penetration testing function. Platforms that enable continuous security validation, such as breach and attack simulation tools, integrate into CI/CD pipelines and provide persistent testing coverage. Cloud-native pen testing tools are designed to assess containers, serverless functions, and ephemeral infrastructure that traditional tools cannot handle effectively. API security testing tools are tailored to the growing reliance on microservices and external integrations. As environments become more dynamic and complex, the tools used by penetration testers must evolve to maintain coverage and relevance.

Governance and compliance frameworks often require organizations to perform regular penetration testing as part of their risk management programs. Integrating pen testing into DevSecOps allows teams to meet these obligations without disrupting delivery. It also improves the quality and reliability of findings by ensuring that tests are performed on up-to-date systems and in environments that closely resemble production. By automating the scheduling, execution, and reporting of tests where possible, organizations reduce the operational burden while increasing coverage and frequency.

The human element remains central to effective penetration testing. While automation can handle scale and speed, it is the skilled tester who discovers subtle flaws, thinks creatively, and understands the broader impact of an exploit. In a DevSecOps model, this expertise is amplified when testers are embedded in teams, participate in design discussions, and collaborate throughout the development lifecycle. Their insights influence not only code but architecture, deployment strategies, and incident response planning.

Penetration testing in DevSecOps is not a one-time exercise or a periodic checkpoint. It is an ongoing, adaptive process that evolves with the application and its environment. It supports early detection of vulnerabilities, continuous risk assessment, and rapid feedback to developers. It enhances collaboration, enforces accountability, and strengthens resilience. By embracing this integrated model, organizations can maintain the speed and agility of DevOps while ensuring that security remains a core element of everything they build and deploy.

Red Teaming and Blue Teaming

Red teaming and blue teaming are foundational practices in cybersecurity that simulate real-world attack and defense scenarios, helping organizations evaluate and improve their security posture in a continuous, practical, and highly effective way. In the context of DevSecOps, these practices take on an even more critical role, aligning offensive and defensive strategies with the fast-paced, automated, and highly integrated development and deployment cycles. As systems evolve and threats become more advanced, red and blue teaming provide a realistic means of testing the resilience of an organization's people, processes, and technologies in ways that traditional assessments cannot.

Red teaming involves simulating the tactics, techniques, and procedures of real-world attackers. A red team operates with the objective of identifying and exploiting vulnerabilities in systems, applications, and operations. These professionals think like adversaries, using a wide range of tools and strategies to bypass controls, gain unauthorized access, escalate privileges, and exfiltrate data. They assess not just technical vulnerabilities, but also human factors, social engineering susceptibility, physical security gaps, and process flaws. The purpose is to reveal what an actual attacker could do and to challenge the assumptions, complacency, and blind spots within an organization's defenses.

Blue teaming, on the other hand, focuses on defending against such attacks. Blue teams monitor networks, systems, and applications for signs of intrusion, misuse, or anomalous behavior. They are responsible for detecting, responding to, and recovering from security incidents. This includes maintaining and tuning security tools such as intrusion detection systems, firewalls, SIEM platforms, and endpoint detection solutions. Blue teams also develop playbooks for incident response, manage threat intelligence, and ensure that log data is collected and analyzed effectively. In a DevSecOps context, blue teams often work closely with development and operations teams to build secure systems from the ground up, ensuring that monitoring, alerting, and response capabilities are integrated into the infrastructure and applications.

The interaction between red and blue teams is what makes this model so valuable. When a red team launches a simulated attack, the blue team is tested on its ability to detect, contain, and respond to the threat. These exercises create a feedback loop in which both teams learn from each other. Red teams learn what techniques are likely to be detected or blocked, and blue teams gain insight into the tactics that adversaries use to bypass defenses. This constant refinement results in a more resilient security posture, where gaps are continuously identified and addressed, and security capabilities evolve to meet new challenges.

In DevSecOps environments, the collaboration between red and blue teams must be agile and iterative. Security is no longer a static set of controls applied after development is complete. It is a continuous process that evolves with each code commit, deployment, and configuration change. Red and blue teaming must adapt to this reality, embedding themselves into the development lifecycle and adjusting their strategies to the pace and complexity of modern software delivery. For red teams, this means designing attack scenarios that reflect the actual architecture, workflows, and tools used by the organization. For blue teams, this means integrating detection mechanisms into CI/CD pipelines, containers, cloud services, and microservices environments.

Purple teaming emerges as a natural extension of this collaboration, where red and blue teams work together intentionally to maximize learning and defensive improvement. In a purple team model, red teams share details about their methods, and blue teams share what they saw or failed to see. They work side by side to develop new detection rules, harden defenses, and automate response actions. This reduces the adversarial tension that sometimes arises in traditional red versus blue exercises and promotes a culture of shared responsibility and continuous improvement. In DevSecOps, where collaboration and communication are essential, purple teaming aligns perfectly with the principles of transparency, agility, and integration.

Realistic red and blue team exercises often go beyond traditional penetration testing or vulnerability scans. They simulate full kill chain scenarios, from reconnaissance and initial access to lateral movement, privilege escalation, and data exfiltration. Red teams may attempt phishing attacks, exploit misconfigurations in cloud services, or abuse exposed APIs. Blue teams, in turn, must detect these signals among a sea of legitimate activity, correlate indicators of compromise, escalate incidents to response teams, and take appropriate containment actions. These simulations provide invaluable insights into detection and response gaps that might otherwise go unnoticed until a real incident occurs.

Metrics are essential to measure the effectiveness of red and blue team activities. Organizations track how long it takes the blue team to detect an intrusion, how quickly they can contain it, and whether they can fully understand and remediate the threat. They also evaluate the red team's success in achieving objectives, remaining undetected, and exploiting weaknesses. These metrics inform strategic decisions, highlight areas for investment, and demonstrate the return on security initiatives. In DevSecOps environments, where speed and visibility are paramount, these measurements provide actionable intelligence that directly supports business goals.

The role of automation in red and blue teaming continues to grow. Red teams leverage automated tools to scan for vulnerabilities, exploit known weaknesses, and mimic attacker behaviors at scale. Blue teams use machine learning and behavioral analytics to identify anomalies, correlate events, and prioritize alerts. Security orchestration tools automate responses to common threats, reducing the time between detection and action. In complex environments, automation ensures that red and blue teams can focus on higher-level strategies while routine tasks are handled efficiently. As environments become more ephemeral, with infrastructure being deployed and destroyed dynamically, automation becomes not only beneficial but necessary to maintain effective offense and defense.

Culture is a critical factor in the success of red and blue teaming. Organizations must foster an environment where findings are welcomed, not feared, and where security is seen as a shared objective rather than an obstacle. Red teams must be empowered to think creatively and challenge assumptions, while blue teams must be supported in their efforts to defend and improve. Leadership must value transparency, continuous learning, and cross-functional collaboration. In DevSecOps, where innovation moves rapidly, security must keep pace without slowing progress. Red and blue teaming, when aligned with these cultural values, becomes a powerful driver of maturity, resilience, and readiness.

Red teaming and blue teaming are no longer just specialized exercises reserved for large enterprises or annual assessments. In the era of DevSecOps, they are ongoing disciplines embedded into the heart of software development and operations. They provide continuous validation of security assumptions, uncover blind spots, and build confidence in the systems being deployed. By integrating red and blue teaming into the DevSecOps lifecycle, organizations transform security from a reactive function into a proactive, adaptive, and strategic capability that strengthens every release, every environment, and every layer of the stack.

Container Orchestration Security

Container orchestration security has become a fundamental concern in modern DevSecOps environments, where scalability, automation, and microservices architecture drive the way applications are developed and deployed. Orchestration platforms like Kubernetes, OpenShift, and Docker Swarm enable organizations to manage containers at scale, handling tasks such as deployment, service discovery, load balancing, auto-scaling, and self-healing. While these platforms provide unmatched flexibility and operational efficiency, they also introduce new layers of complexity that require careful security considerations. Misconfigured clusters, overly permissive access controls, and unmonitored workloads can quickly turn a powerful orchestration platform into an attractive target for attackers.

At the heart of container orchestration security lies the principle of least privilege. Every component in the orchestration environment—from nodes and pods to controllers and service accounts—should operate with only the permissions necessary to perform its function. Kubernetes, the most widely adopted orchestration platform, offers fine-grained access control through Role-Based Access Control (RBAC). By defining roles and binding them to specific users, groups, or service accounts, administrators can ensure that actions like modifying deployments, accessing secrets, or creating resources are only available to trusted identities. However, the default configurations in many environments are often too permissive, allowing access to critical APIs or cluster-wide resources that should be restricted. Properly scoped roles and regular reviews of RBAC policies are essential to prevent privilege escalation and unauthorized access.

Another cornerstone of container orchestration security is securing the control plane. The control plane, which includes the API server, scheduler, controller manager, and etcd database, is the brain of the orchestration platform. If compromised, an attacker can take full control of the entire cluster. Access to the API server must be tightly restricted using TLS encryption, strong authentication methods, and authorization checks. Administrative access should be limited to a small group of trusted individuals, and audit logs should be enabled to track all interactions with the control plane. The etcd datastore, which holds the desired state of the cluster including secrets and configuration data, must also be encrypted at rest and protected from unauthorized access.

The network layer of container orchestration requires robust security mechanisms to prevent unauthorized communication between pods, services, and external systems. By default, many Kubernetes clusters allow unrestricted communication between pods within the same namespace or even across namespaces. This flat network model can lead to lateral movement if an attacker compromises a single pod. Implementing network policies that define which pods are allowed to communicate with each other helps enforce segmentation and reduces the attack surface. These policies can be based on labels, namespaces, or IP blocks and are enforced by network plugins compatible with Kubernetes. In addition, ingress and egress traffic should be controlled using firewalls, service meshes, or web application firewalls to prevent unauthorized access and data exfiltration.

Securing container workloads is another critical aspect of orchestration security. Containers should be built from minimal base images, contain only necessary dependencies, and be regularly scanned for vulnerabilities. Orchestration platforms should be configured to enforce image signing and verification, ensuring that only trusted images are deployed to the cluster. Runtime protections, such as AppArmor, SELinux, or seccomp profiles, can restrict what actions a container can perform, reducing the risk of container escape or exploitation. Kubernetes pod security policies or the newer Pod Security Standards help enforce these restrictions by defining what capabilities containers are allowed to use, whether they can run as root, and what host resources they can access.

Secrets management within the orchestration platform must also be handled with care. Secrets such as API tokens, database credentials, and encryption keys are often used by containerized applications and must be stored securely. Kubernetes provides a native secret management feature, but by default, these secrets are base64-encoded and stored in etcd, which may not be sufficiently secure on its own. Enabling encryption at rest and using access controls for secrets is essential. Many organizations choose to integrate Kubernetes with external secret management systems such as HashiCorp Vault, AWS Secrets Manager, or Azure Key Vault for improved security and auditability. These tools can dynamically generate secrets, rotate them periodically, and limit their lifespan.

Monitoring and observability are crucial for maintaining security in container orchestration environments. Centralized logging and monitoring tools must collect logs from the control plane, worker nodes, containers, and network components. These logs should be analyzed for signs of unusual behavior, failed login attempts, or unauthorized API calls. Integrating this telemetry with a Security Information and Event Management system allows security teams to correlate events, detect intrusions, and respond to threats in real time. Metrics and traces from the orchestration platform provide additional context, enabling teams to detect performance anomalies that might signal resource abuse or denial-of-service attacks.

Configuration management is another area where orchestration platforms are vulnerable if not properly secured. Misconfigured services, overly broad resource permissions, and insecure default settings are common sources of risk. Infrastructure as Code and GitOps workflows allow teams to define, version, and review configuration changes before applying them. Tools that perform policy validation on these configurations ensure that they comply with organizational security standards. For example, policies can prevent the deployment of containers with privileged access, block the use of deprecated APIs, or enforce the use of specific namespaces for production workloads.

Supply chain security is also a growing concern in container orchestration. The images and dependencies used by containers often come from public registries, and attackers have increasingly targeted these registries to distribute malicious packages. Image provenance, signature verification, and the use of private or curated registries help mitigate this risk. Tools that analyze the software bill of materials for each image can detect vulnerable or unapproved components before they are deployed. Automating these checks within the CI/CD pipeline ensures that the orchestration environment is protected from malicious or insecure code as early as possible.

Finally, security must be embedded into the culture and processes of teams that manage orchestration platforms. Training, documentation, and cross-functional collaboration help ensure that developers, DevOps engineers, and security professionals understand how to build and operate secure containerized environments. Threat modeling exercises that consider how attackers might exploit the orchestration layer can inform the design of more resilient systems. Regular audits, compliance assessments, and security reviews help maintain visibility and drive continuous improvement.

Container orchestration security is a dynamic and multifaceted discipline that touches every layer of the cloud-native stack. As orchestration platforms become the backbone of application delivery, securing them is no longer optional. It is a foundational requirement for maintaining trust, resilience, and business continuity in an increasingly automated and interconnected world.

DevSecOps Metrics and KPIs

DevSecOps metrics and key performance indicators are essential tools for understanding, measuring, and improving the effectiveness of integrating security into the software development lifecycle. As organizations move toward a DevSecOps model that emphasizes automation, speed, and collaboration, tracking progress through measurable outcomes becomes vital. Metrics and KPIs allow teams to assess whether security is being consistently and effectively embedded in their workflows, whether vulnerabilities are being identified and addressed promptly, and whether the organization is improving its overall risk posture. They also help leaders make informed decisions, allocate resources effectively, and demonstrate compliance with internal policies and external regulations.

One of the most fundamental metrics in DevSecOps is the number of security vulnerabilities identified over time. This includes vulnerabilities found through static analysis, dynamic testing, dependency scanning, and manual assessments. Tracking these findings helps teams understand the risk landscape and identify patterns that may indicate recurring issues or insecure coding practices. However, the number of vulnerabilities alone is not a sufficient indicator. It must be contextualized with additional data such as severity levels, exploitability, and affected components. A sharp rise in vulnerabilities after introducing a new library or deploying a new service may signal architectural flaws or gaps in the review process. Conversely, a consistent drop in vulnerabilities might indicate that developers are adopting secure coding practices and that preventive controls are working as intended.

Time to remediate is another critical DevSecOps metric. It measures how quickly identified vulnerabilities are fixed and deployed after detection. Faster remediation times indicate that teams are responsive and that security feedback loops are tightly integrated into development workflows. A long time to remediate, especially for high-severity issues, increases the window of exposure and risk. By tracking average remediation times across severity levels, organizations can identify bottlenecks in their patching processes, assess the effectiveness of automation, and prioritize improvements. Time to remediate can also highlight the need for better prioritization tools or improved communication between development and security teams.

Deployment frequency and change failure rate are traditional DevOps metrics that also hold significance in DevSecOps. Deployment frequency reflects how often code is being shipped to production. In secure environments, frequent deployments are only valuable if they are also safe. Monitoring change failure rates helps assess how many deployments introduce security or stability issues. A low change failure rate suggests that security testing and validation are effective, while a high rate may point to inadequate pre-deployment checks or insufficient coverage in test suites. These metrics help reinforce the idea that speed and security must coexist, not compete.

Policy compliance rate is another important metric. In DevSecOps, policies related to access control, encryption, configuration, and data handling are codified and enforced through automated tools. The compliance rate measures how often code, infrastructure, or deployments meet these defined policies. A high compliance rate indicates that teams are following best practices and that automated enforcement is working effectively. A low compliance rate may reflect gaps in training, misalignment between policy and practice, or lack of visibility into compliance requirements. Tracking this metric over time enables organizations to evaluate the adoption of secure development standards and the maturity of their policy-as-code frameworks.

False positives and false negatives in security tools are also worth monitoring. Excessive false positives can lead to alert fatigue, where developers begin to ignore or dismiss security findings. False negatives, on the other hand, represent missed opportunities to catch real vulnerabilities. Tracking the accuracy of security tools helps teams fine-tune configurations, choose better tools, and improve overall signal-to-noise ratio. This is particularly important in automated pipelines where every failed check can block progress, and every missed issue can lead to a breach. Metrics that evaluate the precision and recall of security tools ensure that automation enhances rather than hinders the delivery process.

Coverage metrics provide insight into how comprehensively security is integrated into DevSecOps workflows. This includes the percentage of code repositories with automated scanning enabled, the percentage of builds that include security tests, and the extent of environment coverage for dynamic testing. Higher coverage means a greater portion of the codebase and infrastructure is being evaluated for security risks, reducing the likelihood of blind spots. These metrics can guide investment in tooling, training, and architectural changes to improve overall visibility and control.

Security-related mean time to detect and mean time to respond are operational metrics that assess how quickly threats are identified and mitigated after they occur. While traditionally associated with security operations, these metrics are increasingly relevant in DevSecOps environments where incidents can originate from development, deployment, or misconfiguration. Reducing detection and response times improves resilience and minimizes the impact of security breaches. These metrics also demonstrate the effectiveness of monitoring, logging, and incident response practices that are embedded in DevSecOps workflows.

User engagement with security tooling is another indicator of DevSecOps maturity. This includes how often developers interact with security dashboards, how frequently they review or remediate findings, and whether security alerts are acknowledged and resolved in a timely manner. High engagement suggests that security tools are integrated into daily work and are providing value. Low engagement might indicate that tools are poorly integrated, difficult to use, or misaligned with developer workflows. Measuring and improving engagement helps ensure that security is not seen as an external burden but as a natural and beneficial part of the development process.

Metrics related to secure coding education and awareness can also provide valuable insights. These might include the percentage of developers who have completed security training, the number of security champions embedded within teams, or the number of security-related contributions made during code reviews. These indicators show how well the organization is investing in its human capital and fostering a culture of shared security ownership.

Finally, executive-level KPIs such as risk reduction over time, cost of risk mitigation, and alignment with business objectives help translate technical metrics into strategic value. These KPIs demonstrate how DevSecOps contributes to overall business resilience, customer trust, and regulatory compliance. They enable security leaders to communicate effectively with executive stakeholders and to secure the necessary support for ongoing improvement.

DevSecOps metrics and KPIs are not just numbers. They are reflections of how well an organization has integrated security into its development lifecycle, how effectively it is managing risk, and how successfully it is balancing agility with control. By tracking the right metrics and acting on their insights, teams can continuously improve their processes, deliver more secure software, and build a culture where security is everyone's responsibility.

Security in Serverless Architectures

Security in serverless architectures presents both new opportunities and unique challenges. As organizations continue to adopt serverless computing for its scalability, cost efficiency, and reduced operational overhead, it is essential to recognize that the abstraction of infrastructure does not mean the absence of responsibility. In a serverless environment, cloud providers manage the underlying servers, operating systems, and runtime environments, allowing developers to focus on writing code and deploying functions. While this model shifts certain responsibilities to the provider, the security of the application logic, configuration, data, and access controls remains firmly in the hands of the development and security teams. Understanding these responsibilities and implementing appropriate controls is critical to ensuring that serverless applications remain resilient against threats.

One of the defining features of serverless computing is its event-driven nature. Functions are triggered by events such as HTTP requests, database changes, file uploads, or message queue entries. This increases the potential attack surface, as each event source becomes an entry point that must be secured. For example, an HTTP-triggered function exposed through an API gateway must be protected against injection attacks, cross-site scripting, and rate limiting issues. Similarly, functions triggered by cloud storage uploads must validate the contents of files to prevent malicious payloads. Input validation, strong authentication, and precise authorization checks are fundamental to securing these entry points.

Another critical aspect of serverless security is the principle of least privilege. Each function should operate with the minimal set of permissions required to perform its task. This is managed through fine-grained IAM (Identity and Access Management) policies. In serverless platforms like AWS Lambda, Google Cloud Functions, or Azure Functions, roles can be assigned at the function level, allowing developers to tightly control what resources a function can access. Overly permissive policies, such as granting read-write access to entire databases or storage buckets, increase the risk of data exfiltration if the function is compromised. Regular audits of IAM policies, combined with tools that analyze effective permissions, help maintain a secure permissions model.

The ephemeral nature of serverless functions offers some security benefits, such as reduced persistence for attackers who manage to compromise a function. However, it also introduces challenges in terms of observability and incident response. Traditional endpoint security tools are often incompatible with serverless environments, making it harder to monitor runtime behavior or detect anomalies. This necessitates the use of specialized security tools and logging mechanisms that are designed for serverless. Logging must capture function invocations, input parameters, error messages, and outbound connections. These logs should be sent to centralized systems for analysis and correlated with other data sources to identify suspicious patterns.

Monitoring for excessive invocations or unusual timing patterns can also reveal attempts to exploit a function. Serverless applications are vulnerable to denial-of-wallet attacks, where an attacker deliberately triggers a function repeatedly to increase costs. Implementing throttling, quotas, and billing alerts helps detect and mitigate this type of abuse. Serverless-specific Web Application Firewalls (WAFs) and API gateways that enforce rate limits and inspect traffic can be integrated as front-line defenses to further protect against abuse and common web-based attacks.

Dependency management is another important consideration in serverless security. Most functions rely on external libraries and modules to perform tasks such as parsing JSON, connecting to databases, or handling encryption. These dependencies can introduce known vulnerabilities into the application. Because serverless functions are small and focused, they often include many dependencies in each deployment package. Automated tools should be used to scan these packages for outdated or vulnerable components. Software composition analysis tools can be integrated into the CI/CD pipeline to block deployments that include known issues. Reducing dependency bloat and choosing well-maintained libraries from trusted sources also lowers the risk of including malicious or vulnerable code.

Configuration security plays a vital role in maintaining serverless application integrity. Environment variables are commonly used to store configuration data, including secrets such as API keys and database credentials. These environment variables must be protected to prevent leakage. Secrets should be managed using dedicated secret management services rather than hardcoded into deployment files or function code. Tools like AWS Secrets Manager, Azure Key Vault, or HashiCorp Vault provide secure storage and access control for sensitive data. Functions should retrieve secrets at runtime using encrypted channels and avoid logging sensitive values under any circumstance.

Securing the integration points between serverless functions and other cloud services is equally important. Functions often interact with managed databases, queues, caches, and third-party APIs. Each of these interactions must be secured using appropriate authentication mechanisms, network restrictions, and encryption. For example, serverless functions that access databases should use secure connections with SSL/TLS, and database credentials should be rotated regularly. Where possible, virtual private cloud (VPC) connectivity should be enforced to isolate serverless functions from the public internet and restrict outbound traffic to known destinations.

Continuous security testing is necessary to keep up with the dynamic nature of serverless applications. Unit tests, integration tests, and security tests must all be part of the automated pipeline. Tools that simulate attacks, such as fuzzing or input mutation testing, help identify edge cases where the function may behave unexpectedly. Dynamic Application Security Testing (DAST) tools designed for APIs can evaluate serverless endpoints during deployment stages. Functions should also be tested against compliance policies that reflect organizational standards, such as encryption requirements, naming conventions, or access control rules.

Serverless security also extends to lifecycle management. Functions must be regularly reviewed and decommissioned when no longer in use. Orphaned functions that remain deployed but are no longer actively monitored present significant risks. Attackers can exploit such endpoints if they are forgotten or excluded from logging and alerting systems. Implementing tagging and documentation standards helps track function ownership and usage status. Automation can be used to identify and flag unused functions for review or removal.

The human element remains a key part of securing serverless architectures. Developers must be trained to understand the shared responsibility model, the unique attack vectors in serverless environments, and best practices for writing secure code. Security teams should work alongside developers to provide guidance, tools, and feedback. Security must not be a final checkpoint but a continuous process that is embedded in every phase of the software development lifecycle. In serverless architectures, where agility and abstraction reign, embedding security principles into every layer—from function design to deployment configuration—is the only way to maintain resilience against evolving threats.

Edge Security Considerations

Edge security considerations have become increasingly critical as computing continues to move away from centralized data centers toward distributed edge environments. The rise of edge computing is driven by the need for low-latency processing, real-time analytics, and reduced bandwidth usage. Applications in areas such as autonomous vehicles, smart cities, industrial IoT, and retail rely heavily on processing data closer to where it is generated. While this shift offers performance and operational advantages, it also introduces a new range of security challenges that organizations must address to protect their assets, data, and infrastructure in highly distributed and often physically exposed environments.

Unlike traditional cloud environments, where security can be enforced through centralized controls and monitoring, edge environments operate in a more decentralized and dynamic manner. Edge devices may be deployed in remote locations with limited physical security, intermittent connectivity, and constrained resources. These factors increase the risk of tampering, unauthorized access, data interception, and malware infections. It is essential to approach edge security from a layered perspective, incorporating protections at the hardware, software, network, and data layers.

Physical security is the first and most basic concern at the edge. Devices deployed in outdoor, industrial, or unattended locations are vulnerable to theft, destruction, or physical tampering. Unlike data center hardware, which is protected by access controls and surveillance, edge devices might be installed on lamp posts, inside vehicles, or within factory equipment. Organizations must ensure that these devices are tamper-resistant, use secure enclosures, and trigger alerts when unauthorized physical access is detected. Hardware security modules or trusted platform modules can be used to securely store cryptographic keys and perform sensitive operations in a protected environment, even if the rest of the system is compromised.

Authentication and identity management are also critical at the edge. Each edge device must have a unique, verifiable identity to participate securely in the broader ecosystem. This identity should be provisioned during manufacturing or initial configuration and should be immutable or at least verifiable through cryptographic means. Mutual authentication between edge devices and central services ensures that only trusted components can communicate with each other. Public key infrastructure or certificate-based authentication schemes are common approaches, but they must be designed to accommodate the scale and connectivity constraints of edge environments.

Secure boot and firmware validation are essential to ensure that edge devices are running only trusted and verified software. Secure boot processes validate digital signatures on firmware images before execution, preventing the execution of unauthorized or malicious code. Firmware should be signed by the device manufacturer or an authorized party and stored in protected memory. Regular firmware updates are necessary to patch vulnerabilities and enhance functionality, but the update process itself must be secure. Over-the-air update mechanisms should use encrypted channels, authenticate update sources, and validate signatures before applying changes. Failure to secure the firmware lifecycle can result in widespread compromise across fleets of edge devices.

Communication security at the edge is another major concern. Data transmitted between edge devices, gateways, and central systems must be encrypted to prevent interception, tampering, and replay attacks. Transport Layer Security or equivalent protocols should be used consistently, even on constrained devices. In environments with intermittent connectivity, data may be stored locally before transmission, which introduces the need for data-at-rest encryption. Keys used for encryption and authentication must be rotated regularly and managed securely, ideally using automated key management systems that minimize manual intervention and reduce the risk of exposure.

Network segmentation and isolation are necessary to reduce the attack surface of edge environments. Devices should not be allowed to communicate freely with every other component on the network. Instead, access should be controlled through firewalls, virtual networks, or software-defined perimeter solutions. Segmentation limits the potential impact of compromised devices and prevents lateral movement by attackers. In larger edge deployments, micro-segmentation may be used to define communication policies at a granular level, ensuring that devices and services only interact when necessary and only through approved pathways.

Monitoring and logging are especially challenging in edge environments due to bandwidth limitations and the sheer volume of distributed components. Nevertheless, visibility into edge operations is critical for detecting anomalies, investigating incidents, and maintaining compliance. Logs and telemetry should be stored locally and periodically forwarded to central systems for analysis. Edge-specific SIEM integrations and lightweight monitoring agents can help identify unusual behaviors, such as unexpected firmware changes, excessive network activity, or repeated authentication failures. Event correlation across multiple edge sites enables organizations to detect coordinated attacks and respond quickly.

Data privacy and compliance are growing concerns at the edge, particularly when sensitive information is collected and processed locally. Regulations such as GDPR, HIPAA, and industry-specific standards place strict requirements on how data is handled. Edge solutions must incorporate privacy-by-design principles, such as data minimization, anonymization, and local processing where feasible. Data collected at the edge should be evaluated for its sensitivity and classified accordingly, with stronger protections applied to regulated or personally identifiable information. Access to this data must be restricted, audited, and governed by policy.

Security automation and orchestration are essential for managing the scale and complexity of edge deployments. Manual configuration and management are not feasible when thousands of devices are deployed across diverse geographic locations. Tools that automate provisioning, policy enforcement, patching, and security updates reduce the burden on operational teams and ensure consistency. Centralized orchestration platforms can push security policies to edge devices, monitor compliance, and initiate remediation actions when violations are detected. These platforms must be resilient to network outages and capable of synchronizing state when connectivity is restored.

Threat modeling is a valuable practice in designing edge security strategies. By identifying potential attack vectors, adversary capabilities, and system vulnerabilities, teams can prioritize defenses and allocate resources effectively. Scenarios such as physical device compromise, man-in-the-middle attacks, rogue firmware, and denial-of-service attempts must be considered. Threat modeling should account for the entire edge-to-cloud lifecycle, including device provisioning, operational use, and decommissioning. Security controls should be layered and redundant, ensuring that no single point of failure can compromise the system.

Human factors play a significant role in edge security. Devices are often installed and maintained by personnel who may not have specialized security training. Clear guidelines, training programs, and user-friendly interfaces can help prevent misconfigurations and reduce human error. Role-based access controls and least-privilege principles should govern who can access or modify edge systems. In environments where third-party contractors or partners interact with edge infrastructure, strict onboarding, monitoring, and revocation procedures are necessary.

Edge computing expands the reach and power of digital systems, bringing intelligence and responsiveness closer to where data is generated. With that power comes a heightened responsibility to secure a more complex and distributed environment. Addressing edge security considerations requires a holistic approach that spans hardware, software, network, identity, and data protection. By implementing robust security practices tailored to the unique characteristics of edge computing, organizations can fully realize its benefits while mitigating the risks that come with operating at the frontier of digital infrastructure.

DevSecOps for Mobile Applications

DevSecOps for mobile applications introduces a unique set of challenges and considerations that differ from traditional web or desktop software development. Mobile apps operate in a highly dynamic ecosystem that includes various operating systems, device models, hardware capabilities, and distribution mechanisms. In this environment, ensuring security is not only about protecting the backend services and APIs but also securing the application on the device itself, the data it handles, and the communication it initiates. As mobile applications continue to expand their presence in sectors such as finance, healthcare, and e-commerce, the need for a DevSecOps approach tailored to mobile becomes increasingly urgent. Integrating security into the entire lifecycle of mobile app development—from planning to deployment and monitoring—ensures that security is proactive, continuous, and aligned with rapid release cycles.

The first layer of mobile application security in a DevSecOps framework starts during the design and planning stages. Security considerations must be embedded in the architecture from the outset. Threat modeling is a critical practice during this phase. It helps identify potential attack vectors, such as insecure data storage, exposed APIs, improper authentication, or reliance on outdated third-party libraries. For mobile apps, specific threats such as reverse engineering, code tampering, and unauthorized access to device resources must be evaluated and mitigated through strategic design choices. This proactive approach prevents vulnerabilities from being introduced in the first place and ensures that developers are building with security in mind.

Source code security plays a pivotal role in mobile DevSecOps. Developers must follow secure coding practices and be trained to recognize risky patterns, particularly those common in mobile environments such as storing sensitive data in plain text or logging personal information. Mobile applications are susceptible to reverse engineering, especially on platforms like Android where APK files can be easily decompiled. To combat this, developers must apply techniques like code obfuscation, certificate pinning, and runtime integrity checks. These measures increase the difficulty for attackers attempting to analyze or modify the application. Static application security testing tools specifically designed for mobile can be integrated into the CI/CD pipeline to automatically scan code for vulnerabilities and coding flaws as it is committed.

Managing third-party libraries and dependencies is another critical aspect of DevSecOps for mobile apps. Most mobile applications rely on external SDKs and libraries to provide functionality such as analytics, payment processing, or social media integration. These dependencies can introduce vulnerabilities if not regularly updated or sourced from trusted providers. Software composition analysis tools should be employed to track the origin, version, and vulnerability status of every third-party component. Insecure or outdated libraries must be flagged and replaced before they reach production. Regular reviews of the dependency tree and automated alerts for newly discovered CVEs help maintain a secure codebase.

Data protection is particularly challenging in mobile apps due to the nature of user devices and varying levels of control. Mobile apps often store data locally, whether in files, preferences, or databases. Developers must ensure that any sensitive data stored on the device is encrypted using strong, platform-approved methods. Additionally, proper access controls must be enforced to prevent data leaks across apps or users. For example, data stored in shared storage should be carefully restricted, and backup exclusions should be applied to prevent sensitive files from being uploaded to cloud backup services. On-device encryption and secure storage APIs provided by platforms such as Android Keystore and Apple's Keychain should be leveraged wherever possible.

Authentication and session management must be implemented securely to prevent unauthorized access. Mobile applications should use secure token-based authentication mechanisms, such as OAuth2 or OpenID Connect, rather than relying on traditional username-password authentication stored locally. Session tokens should be short-lived, rotated regularly, and stored securely. The use of biometric authentication, where supported, can enhance security while improving user experience. Developers must also guard against token leakage through logs, screenshots, or improper error messages. Multi-factor authentication should be offered for applications handling sensitive or financial information, with careful handling of push-based verification and timeout mechanisms.

Secure communication is non-negotiable in mobile apps, as they constantly transmit data over public networks. All data in transit must be encrypted using TLS, and developers should enforce the use of modern TLS versions while disabling insecure protocols and cipher suites. Certificate pinning can be implemented to prevent man-in-the-middle attacks, although it must be done cautiously to avoid breaking functionality during certificate renewal. Mobile apps should never transmit sensitive information over HTTP or store sensitive data in URLs or query parameters. Penetration tests that focus on communication channels are essential for identifying misconfigurations and vulnerabilities that static analysis might miss.

Continuous integration and continuous delivery pipelines must be adapted for mobile-specific workflows. This includes automated builds for multiple device platforms, automated UI testing on device farms, and integration of security tools that target mobile environments. Dynamic application security testing should be applied to staging builds, where automated scripts simulate user behavior to uncover runtime vulnerabilities. Test automation helps ensure that security checks are not sacrificed for speed, and the use of emulators and real devices in parallel helps improve test coverage across different OS versions and hardware capabilities.

Distribution and deployment bring another layer of complexity to mobile DevSecOps. Apps are typically distributed through app stores, which introduce their own validation and security requirements. However, these marketplaces are not foolproof and should not be relied upon as the sole line of defense. Organizations must sign their applications with secure certificates, manage key lifecycles carefully, and monitor for unauthorized copies or clones of their apps on unofficial app stores. Mobile application protection solutions can be used to detect tampering, enable remote disablement, and monitor for suspicious behavior in the wild.

Monitoring and feedback loops close the DevSecOps cycle for mobile apps. Telemetry collected from mobile applications in production can provide valuable insights into security-related behavior. Crash logs, permission usage statistics, and network activity can be analyzed to detect anomalies or signals of potential compromise. When paired with mobile RASP (Runtime Application Self-Protection) technologies, apps can detect and respond to threats in real time, such as debugging attempts or root detection. These insights must be funneled back into development, allowing teams to patch, improve, and harden future releases based on real-world data.

DevSecOps for mobile applications is a continuous effort that requires deep integration of security into every phase of the mobile development lifecycle. The rapidly evolving nature of mobile platforms, combined with a growing threat landscape, demands vigilance, automation, and collaboration across teams. By adopting a DevSecOps mindset tailored for mobile, organizations can build secure, resilient, and user-friendly applications that stand up to the challenges of modern mobile computing.

DevSecOps for Web Applications

DevSecOps for web applications is the process of embedding security into every phase of the web application development lifecycle. In today's digital landscape, where web applications serve as the primary interface between users and businesses, security cannot be an afterthought. The speed and flexibility of DevOps have revolutionized how applications are built and deployed, but without integrating security into these pipelines, vulnerabilities can be introduced and released to production faster than ever before. DevSecOps ensures that security becomes an inherent part of the development culture, automating security checks and empowering teams to detect, fix, and prevent vulnerabilities from the first line of code to the final deployment.

The unique nature of web applications requires a specific set of security considerations. Unlike mobile or desktop applications, web applications are constantly exposed to the internet and are frequent targets for attackers. They must handle user input, interact with backend services, store and process sensitive data, and maintain availability even under attack. A DevSecOps approach to web application security begins at the design phase, where security requirements must be identified alongside business and functional requirements. Threat modeling is an essential practice at this stage. It helps teams anticipate potential threats, such as injection attacks, broken access controls, cross-site scripting, and insecure deserialization, and implement mitigation strategies before coding begins.

Once development begins, secure coding practices are critical. Developers must be trained to avoid common mistakes that lead to vulnerabilities, such as failing to sanitize input, improper error handling, and using outdated or insecure libraries. To support developers, static application security testing tools can be integrated into the CI pipeline. These tools scan the source code or bytecode for known vulnerability patterns and provide immediate feedback. This early detection allows developers to fix issues while the code is still fresh in their minds, significantly reducing the cost and effort of remediation. It also helps create a culture where security is treated as part of quality, not a separate concern.

Web applications often rely on third-party libraries and frameworks for functionality. These dependencies can introduce vulnerabilities if not carefully managed. Software composition analysis tools should be used to scan dependencies for known vulnerabilities and licensing issues. These tools continuously monitor public databases such as the National Vulnerability Database and alert teams when a vulnerable component is discovered in their codebase. Keeping dependencies up to date and maintaining a trusted list of approved packages reduces the risk of supply chain attacks and ensures that security patches are applied promptly.

During the build and testing stages, dynamic application security testing plays a vital role. Unlike static analysis, which focuses on code, dynamic testing simulates real user interactions with the running application to identify issues that arise only at runtime. DAST tools can detect problems like authentication bypass, logic flaws, and session management weaknesses. These tools should be included in automated testing pipelines, especially for staging environments, to ensure that each release is evaluated against a comprehensive set of security criteria. Web application firewalls can be configured to work with DAST tools, simulating attack traffic and helping teams tune detection and prevention rules.

Infrastructure and configuration also play a major role in web application security. DevSecOps requires that infrastructure be treated as code, using tools like Terraform, Ansible, or Kubernetes manifests to define and manage the environments where web applications run. These definitions must be scanned for misconfigurations, such as open ports, weak authentication, or exposed administrative interfaces. Policy-as-code frameworks can enforce security standards automatically, blocking deployments that do not meet the organization's security requirements. This proactive validation prevents unsafe environments from reaching production and ensures consistency across staging, testing, and live systems.

Secrets management is a critical aspect of secure web application development. Web apps often require access to databases, APIs, and third-party services, all of which require credentials. These secrets must never be hardcoded or stored in version control. Instead, secrets should be managed using secure vaults and injected into runtime environments using encrypted channels. Role-based access control should govern who can view, edit, or use these secrets. Auditing capabilities in secret management systems help track usage and detect misuse, while automated rotation of secrets reduces the risk of long-term exposure.

Deployment and release processes in DevSecOps for web applications must also prioritize security. Continuous delivery pipelines should include gates that prevent the promotion of builds containing critical vulnerabilities. Approvals and sign-offs can be automated or manual, depending on the risk profile of the application and the environment. Blue-green deployments, canary releases, and feature flags allow teams to release new functionality gradually, monitor for anomalies, and roll back changes quickly if issues are detected. These strategies enhance both security and reliability, providing controlled environments for validating security controls under real-world conditions.

Once deployed, monitoring and incident response become the focus. Web applications must be continuously observed for signs of attack, compromise, or misuse. Logging should capture relevant events such as login attempts, permission changes, data access, and error messages. Logs must be forwarded to centralized systems and retained securely for analysis. Integrating these logs with a SIEM platform enables real-time correlation of events, alerting security teams to potential incidents. Monitoring tools should also track application performance and behavior, as sudden spikes in CPU usage, memory consumption, or network traffic may indicate an attack.

Regular security assessments, including penetration testing and red teaming, should be performed to validate the effectiveness of

DevSecOps controls. These assessments simulate real-world attack scenarios and identify vulnerabilities that automated tools might miss. Findings from these exercises should be prioritized based on risk, with remediation tasks tracked in the same systems used by developers. Blameless postmortems after incidents or assessments help teams learn and improve without fear of punishment, fostering a culture of accountability and continuous improvement.

DevSecOps for web applications requires a shift in mindset, tools, and collaboration. It demands that security be built into every phase of development and not treated as an afterthought or final checkpoint. It requires that developers, operations, and security professionals work together, using shared tools, metrics, and goals to deliver secure applications at speed. The result is not only more secure web applications but also more resilient teams and systems that can adapt to evolving threats. As the web continues to be the primary interface for digital interaction, DevSecOps ensures that organizations can innovate with confidence, knowing that security is a continuous, integrated, and automated part of their success.

Integrating DevSecOps in Legacy Systems

Integrating DevSecOps into legacy systems is a complex but necessary undertaking for organizations aiming to modernize their software development lifecycle without completely abandoning their existing infrastructure. These older systems, often referred to as legacy due to their age or outdated technology stack, still serve critical business functions. They are typically stable, heavily customized, and deeply embedded within an organization's operational fabric. However, they often lack the agility, automation, and security measures found in modern cloud-native environments. As cyber threats become more sophisticated and the demand for faster, more secure software delivery increases, the need to embed security into every phase of the development and operations pipeline becomes undeniable—even for legacy systems.

The process begins with understanding the architecture and constraints of the legacy environment. Unlike modern microservices-based systems, legacy applications are frequently monolithic, meaning that any change, even a minor one, can have far-reaching consequences. Therefore, one of the first steps in integrating DevSecOps is to map out the application's dependencies, identify security gaps, and prioritize areas where automation and security improvements can be introduced with minimal disruption. This often requires close collaboration between development, security, and operations teams, as well as input from business stakeholders who understand the critical functionality that must remain intact.

One of the primary challenges in this integration is the lack of support for modern tooling. Legacy systems may not be compatible with contemporary continuous integration and continuous deployment (CI/CD) platforms, or they may be hosted on outdated operating systems that do not support the latest security standards. In such cases, organizations must get creative, leveraging middleware, wrappers, or custom scripts to bridge the gap between old and new. For instance, while a legacy application might not support containerization, components surrounding it—such as monitoring, logging, and vulnerability scanning—can be containerized or modernized to improve security and visibility. This hybrid approach allows teams to reap some of the benefits of DevSecOps without having to rewrite the entire application from scratch.

Automation plays a crucial role in the success of this transformation. By automating repetitive tasks such as code scanning, dependency checks, configuration validation, and patch management, teams can reduce human error and accelerate the deployment pipeline. However, automation must be introduced carefully and incrementally in legacy environments. Too much automation too quickly can destabilize a fragile system. Instead, organizations often start by automating security checks in the development or staging environments, gradually expanding the scope to include testing, integration, and eventually production deployments. This progressive rollout helps build confidence and allows for continuous learning and adjustment.

Security integration must be treated as a shared responsibility, and legacy systems often suffer from a siloed culture where developers, operations, and security teams work in isolation. DevSecOps demands a cultural shift toward collaboration, transparency, and accountability. In legacy environments, this means breaking down these silos and encouraging cross-functional teams to work together from the earliest phases of development. Security must no longer be an afterthought or a checkpoint at the end of the release cycle; it needs to be woven into the fabric of the software development process. This mindset shift is perhaps one of the most difficult but most critical aspects of integrating DevSecOps.

Metrics and monitoring are also key components of a successful DevSecOps strategy in legacy environments. Teams need visibility into application performance, security events, and deployment activities to make informed decisions. Legacy systems often lack robust monitoring tools, so part of the integration process involves retrofitting or augmenting these systems with modern observability solutions. This might include introducing agents for log collection, implementing intrusion detection systems, or configuring alerting mechanisms for unusual activity. The data collected from these systems not only helps in responding to incidents but also in proactively identifying and mitigating potential risks.

Governance and compliance cannot be overlooked, especially in regulated industries where legacy systems are most prevalent. These systems often handle sensitive data and are subject to strict regulatory standards. Integrating DevSecOps must therefore include mechanisms to ensure auditability, traceability, and adherence to compliance requirements. This can be achieved through automated policy enforcement, detailed logging, and regular audits of both the codebase and the deployment processes. Documentation becomes crucial in these environments, serving as a bridge between evolving technical practices and established regulatory expectations.

Training and upskilling are equally important. Many professionals who work on legacy systems are highly experienced but may not be familiar with DevSecOps principles or tools. Providing them with hands-on training, mentorship opportunities, and exposure to modern practices helps ensure that the integration effort is sustainable. Organizations that invest in their people often find that resistance to change decreases, and adoption of new methodologies becomes smoother. It also helps to celebrate small wins, such as the successful automation of a manual process or the integration of a new security tool, to build momentum and foster a sense of progress.

Despite the challenges, integrating DevSecOps into legacy systems is not only possible but increasingly essential. As threats evolve and digital transformation accelerates, clinging to outdated development and security practices puts organizations at risk. By adopting a pragmatic, incremental approach—one that respects the constraints of legacy systems while embracing the benefits of DevSecOps—organizations can enhance their security posture, increase operational efficiency, and extend the life and value of their legacy assets. The journey may be long and occasionally difficult, but the rewards of a more secure, agile, and resilient software environment make it a worthwhile endeavor.

Cloud-Native Security Practices

Cloud-native security practices are essential in today's software development landscape, where applications are designed to run in dynamic, distributed environments such as public, private, or hybrid clouds. These practices are not mere extensions of traditional security models but rather a complete rethinking of how security is implemented in systems that rely on containers, microservices, orchestration platforms like Kubernetes, and continuous integration and delivery pipelines. The nature of cloud-native architectures—ephemeral, scalable, and service-oriented—requires a security approach that is automated, integrated, and deeply embedded in the development lifecycle.

One of the foundational aspects of cloud-native security is the principle of zero trust. Unlike legacy networks that relied heavily on perimeter-based defenses, zero trust assumes that threats may originate from inside or outside the network and therefore requires verification at every layer. This means identity and access management (IAM) becomes a cornerstone of security. In cloud-native environments, every user, service, and process must be authenticated and authorized using fine-grained policies. Roles and permissions must be tightly controlled using least-privilege principles, ensuring that entities have only the minimum access necessary to perform their functions.

Another critical component of cloud-native security is automation. The fast-paced nature of cloud-native development, where deployments happen several times a day, demands security controls that can keep up. Manual processes simply do not scale. Security as code becomes a powerful paradigm here, enabling teams to define and enforce security policies in the same way they manage application code. Infrastructure as code (IaC) tools such as Terraform or CloudFormation allow teams to create secure environments programmatically, while security scanning tools can automatically inspect configurations for misconfigurations or policy violations before anything goes live.

Containers and microservices bring their own unique security challenges and opportunities. Since containers package code with all its dependencies, vulnerabilities in base images or third-party libraries can be replicated across multiple instances. To mitigate this, container images must be regularly scanned for vulnerabilities, and only signed, verified images should be allowed to run in production. Image registries need to be tightly controlled, and policies should prevent the use of outdated or unverified images. Runtime security also plays a crucial role. Monitoring container behavior to detect anomalies, such as unexpected system calls or network connections, can help identify compromised services before significant damage is done.

Kubernetes, as the de facto orchestration platform for cloud-native applications, also demands specialized security practices. Its complexity can lead to misconfigurations that expose services or allow unauthorized access. Role-based access control (RBAC) must be properly implemented to limit what users and services can do within the cluster. Network policies should be defined to control traffic flow between pods, and secrets management should be handled securely using tools that integrate with Kubernetes' native capabilities or external systems like HashiCorp Vault. Regular audits and validation of cluster configurations are necessary to ensure compliance with organizational security standards.

DevSecOps plays a vital role in ensuring that security is not an afterthought but an integral part of the development pipeline. Security checks must be embedded at every stage—from writing code to deploying applications. Static code analysis, dependency scanning, and dynamic application security testing help identify issues early in the lifecycle, when they are cheaper and easier to fix. By integrating these tools into CI/CD pipelines, teams can achieve continuous security without slowing down development. Additionally, feedback loops ensure that developers are informed immediately of any issues, enabling quick resolution and fostering a culture of shared responsibility for security.

Observability and incident response are also essential components of cloud-native security. Given the ephemeral nature of containers and dynamic scaling of services, traditional logging and monitoring methods may fall short. Cloud-native systems require centralized logging, metrics collection, and distributed tracing to provide real-time insights into application behavior and performance. Tools such as Prometheus, Grafana, Fluentd, and OpenTelemetry offer ways to collect and analyze data across the entire stack. Alerts and dashboards must be configured to detect signs of compromise, performance degradation, or policy violations. When incidents do occur, teams must have well-defined response playbooks that include isolation of affected components, rollback procedures, and post-mortem analysis to prevent recurrence.

Another important aspect is compliance and governance. Many organizations operate in industries with strict regulatory requirements such as healthcare, finance, or government. Cloud-native security must support these compliance efforts through automated policy enforcement, detailed auditing, and continuous monitoring. Tools that provide policy-as-code capabilities, such as Open Policy Agent (OPA) or Kyverno, allow teams to codify governance rules and apply them consistently across environments. Compliance frameworks like SOC 2, HIPAA, or GDPR can be mapped to technical controls, making it easier to demonstrate adherence through automated reporting and evidence collection.

One of the less technical but equally important facets of cloud-native security is fostering a security-first culture. This involves educating development teams about common threats, secure coding practices, and the importance of keeping security in mind throughout the development process. Security champions programs, where developers take on the additional responsibility of advocating for security within their teams, have proven effective in bridging the gap between security specialists and engineering teams. Cross-functional collaboration ensures that security concerns are addressed early and not simply handed off to a separate team at the end of a project.

As organizations continue to move toward cloud-native architectures, the importance of adopting modern security practices cannot be overstated. The agility, scalability, and resilience offered by the cloud can only be fully realized if security is treated as a first-class citizen. By embedding security into every layer of the stack, automating processes wherever possible, and fostering a culture of continuous improvement, organizations can build systems that are not only fast and flexible but also robust and secure.

Managing Secrets in Cloud Environments

Managing secrets in cloud environments has become a critical discipline in modern software development and infrastructure management. Secrets—such as API keys, database credentials, encryption keys, and tokens—are essential for applications to function, but they also represent high-value targets for attackers. In cloud-native environments where resources are dynamic, services are ephemeral, and infrastructure is defined as code, the traditional methods of managing secrets no longer suffice. Storing secrets in configuration files, environment variables, or source code repositories exposes organizations to significant security risks, making it essential to adopt robust, automated, and scalable secrets management practices.

Cloud environments introduce new complexities in the way secrets are created, accessed, and rotated. Unlike static data centers with long-lived servers and manual configurations, cloud-native architectures rely on automation and rapid provisioning. Virtual machines, containers, and serverless functions can be spun up and down in seconds, which requires a different approach to securely distributing and managing secrets. Static secrets or hardcoded credentials quickly become liabilities, especially when they are difficult to rotate or revoke. Secrets must be treated as dynamic resources that are short-lived, scoped appropriately, and accessible only to authorized entities.

The foundation of secure secret management begins with centralized secret storage. Rather than distributing secrets across configuration files or multiple services, organizations should consolidate secrets into a dedicated secrets manager. Cloud providers offer native solutions such as AWS Secrets Manager, Azure Key Vault, and Google Secret Manager, while third-party tools like HashiCorp Vault and CyberArk offer more advanced features for complex, hybrid, or multi-cloud environments. These tools provide a secure, encrypted store for sensitive information, as well as fine-grained access controls, detailed auditing, and support for dynamic secrets. Centralized management also simplifies operations, allowing teams to automate secret generation, expiration, and revocation.

Access to secrets must be governed by strict policies based on the principle of least privilege. Only the entities that absolutely require access to a secret should be granted permission, and that access should be limited to the minimum scope and duration necessary. This can be achieved by integrating secrets management with the cloud provider's identity and access management (IAM) system. Services, applications, and users are granted roles that determine which secrets they can access, and under what conditions. This approach allows for better tracking and control, as well as the ability to revoke access quickly if credentials are compromised or no longer needed.

Automation is another vital aspect of managing secrets effectively in the cloud. Manual handling of secrets is not only error-prone but also incompatible with the scale and speed of cloud-native systems. Automated workflows ensure that secrets are injected into applications at runtime, rather than baked into images or code. For example, orchestration platforms like Kubernetes support integrations with secret management tools, enabling applications to mount secrets as volumes or expose them as environment variables in a secure and temporary manner. These secrets can be rotated automatically without requiring a redeployment of the application, reducing downtime and the risk of human error.

Secret rotation is a best practice that significantly reduces the potential damage from a leaked or compromised credential. Instead of relying on long-lived secrets that persist for weeks or months, organizations should adopt policies that enforce frequent rotation. Many secrets management tools support dynamic secrets, which are generated on demand and expire after a predefined time or use. For example, a database credential might be created when an application starts, used for a single session, and then automatically revoked. This model limits the window of opportunity for attackers and eliminates the need to manually rotate secrets across hundreds of services and environments.

Auditability and monitoring are essential to maintaining visibility into how secrets are used across the organization. Secrets managers typically generate logs for every access request, change, or policy update, allowing security teams to detect suspicious behavior and enforce compliance. These logs should be integrated with centralized logging and security information and event management (SIEM) systems to provide real-time insights and alerts. For instance, if an application suddenly accesses a large number of secrets, or if an unusual pattern of access is detected outside of business hours, these events can trigger investigations or automated remediation workflows.

Secrets management must also be considered in the context of DevOps and continuous integration/continuous deployment (CI/CD) pipelines. Developers and automation tools often require access to secrets to build, test, and deploy applications. However, embedding secrets directly into CI/CD scripts or storing them in plaintext in version control systems is a dangerous practice. Instead, secrets should be stored in vaults and accessed dynamically during the pipeline execution. Many secrets management tools provide plugins or API integrations with popular CI/CD platforms, ensuring that secrets are delivered securely, used only when necessary, and never exposed in logs or artifacts.

Education and awareness are crucial in building a culture that prioritizes secure secrets management. Developers, DevOps engineers, and system administrators must understand the risks associated with poor secret handling and the benefits of following best practices. Organizations should implement policies and training programs that emphasize secure coding, proper use of secret management tools, and incident response procedures for leaked credentials. Encouraging a proactive approach and providing easy-to-use tools helps reduce the likelihood of shortcuts or misconfigurations that could expose sensitive data.

Finally, managing secrets in cloud environments is not a one-time project but an ongoing effort. As systems evolve, new services are added, and threats continue to emerge, secret management strategies must be revisited and updated regularly. Security teams should conduct periodic reviews of access policies, rotate long-lived secrets, and ensure that deprecated credentials are removed promptly. A successful secrets management strategy is one that evolves alongside the organization, seamlessly integrating into the development lifecycle and supporting the agility of modern cloud-native applications while maintaining a strong security posture.

Continuous Risk Assessment

Continuous risk assessment is a fundamental practice in modern cybersecurity strategies, especially in dynamic, cloud-native, and DevOps-driven environments. Unlike traditional risk assessments that are performed periodically—often once a year or before a major deployment—continuous risk assessment embraces the constantly changing nature of digital systems. It recognizes that threats evolve rapidly, configurations drift, and software is deployed at increasing speed. Therefore, risk management must become a living, breathing part of the development and operations lifecycle, embedded into every stage of the system's existence rather than treated as a static compliance checkpoint.

The goal of continuous risk assessment is to maintain an up-to-date understanding of an organization's threat landscape, vulnerabilities, and potential impacts. This real-time awareness enables teams to make informed decisions, prioritize remediation efforts, and reduce exposure before adversaries can exploit weaknesses. To achieve this, continuous risk assessment must be automated, scalable, and integrated across the entire technology stack—from code repositories and cloud infrastructure to runtime environments and user endpoints. It is a comprehensive approach that requires collaboration across security, development, operations, and business units to ensure that risk is contextualized, relevant, and actionable.

A critical enabler of continuous risk assessment is the use of automated tools that continuously scan and analyze systems for vulnerabilities, misconfigurations, and indicators of compromise. These tools feed into dashboards and risk engines that calculate risk scores, helping organizations quantify their exposure in terms of likelihood and impact. Vulnerability scanners, configuration management tools, static and dynamic code analyzers, and cloud security posture management platforms work together to provide a holistic view of the organization's risk posture. The outputs from these tools must be normalized and correlated to identify patterns and prioritize the most pressing issues, rather than flooding security teams with a barrage of alerts.

Context is essential in evaluating risk accurately. Not all vulnerabilities pose the same level of threat, and not all assets carry the same level of importance. Continuous risk assessment platforms must be able to take into account business context, asset criticality, threat intelligence, and the likelihood of exploitation. For example, a vulnerability in an externally exposed web application that handles financial data is far more severe than the same issue in an internal test system. By weighting risk according to business impact and threat likelihood, organizations can ensure that their limited resources are directed toward the issues that matter most.

Risk assessment must extend into the development lifecycle, starting as early as possible in the software delivery process. Developers should receive feedback about potential risks as they write code, not after the application is deployed. Integrating static application security testing (SAST) and software composition analysis (SCA) into integrated development environments (IDEs) and CI/CD pipelines helps identify insecure code, outdated dependencies, and licensing issues early on. These early-stage insights feed into the continuous risk model, allowing teams to address issues proactively. When risks are mitigated before they reach production, the cost of remediation is significantly lower and the organization's overall security posture is stronger.

Configuration management is another critical area for continuous risk monitoring. Cloud environments, infrastructure as code, and container orchestration platforms allow for rapid changes in system configurations. However, with this speed comes the risk of misconfigurations, which are among the leading causes of security breaches in cloud environments. Continuous assessment tools must monitor infrastructure as code templates, cloud service configurations, and access controls to detect drift from security best practices. When changes are detected—such as the exposure of a storage bucket or the elevation of privileges—they must be flagged and remediated immediately to prevent potential exploitation.

Threat intelligence plays a significant role in contextualizing risk in real time. By integrating threat feeds into risk assessment platforms, organizations can correlate known threats with their internal environments. For instance, if a new zero-day vulnerability is reported in a popular library used by a critical application, the risk assessment system can flag the affected systems, assign a high priority score, and notify relevant stakeholders. This enables teams to respond before attackers can act. Threat intelligence also helps organizations stay ahead of emerging risks by providing insights into attacker tactics, techniques, and procedures.

User behavior analytics and access monitoring contribute to the continuous understanding of insider and external threats. Monitoring who accesses what, when, and how can reveal anomalies that suggest compromised credentials, malicious insiders, or accidental misuse. Risk models can incorporate these signals to adjust risk scores dynamically and trigger appropriate responses. For example, a sudden login from an unusual location or the download of large volumes of sensitive data might increase the risk profile of a user or system, prompting further investigation or the automatic enforcement of security controls.

Reporting and visualization are vital to making continuous risk assessment actionable. Security and business leaders need clear, real-time insights into the organization's risk exposure. Dashboards that display risk scores, trends over time, and progress toward remediation goals help align technical efforts with business objectives. These tools also aid in communication with stakeholders, auditors, and regulators by providing evidence of a proactive, continuous risk management strategy. Furthermore, by tracking key performance indicators (KPIs) and key risk indicators (KRIs), organizations can assess the effectiveness of their risk management programs and identify areas for improvement.

As environments grow more complex and interconnected, continuous risk assessment is evolving from a security function into a business imperative. Organizations that can adapt quickly to new threats, respond to vulnerabilities in real time, and maintain a clear picture of their risk landscape are better positioned to protect their assets and maintain customer trust. This approach supports not just security, but resilience, agility, and informed decision-making across the enterprise. By embracing continuous risk assessment as a foundational practice, organizations build a culture where security is not just a destination, but an integral, ongoing process that evolves in lockstep with technology and business innovation.

Business Continuity and Resilience

Business continuity and resilience are essential pillars of a robust organizational strategy in the face of increasing cyber threats, global disruptions, and complex technological dependencies. As businesses become more reliant on digital infrastructure, the risks associated with downtime, data loss, and operational disruption have grown significantly. Organizations must not only plan for emergencies but also design systems and processes that can withstand unexpected shocks and continue to deliver critical functions. Business continuity ensures that an organization can maintain essential operations during a crisis, while resilience focuses on the ability to adapt, recover, and emerge stronger from disruptions. Together, they form a proactive framework that enables long-term stability and trust.

At the heart of business continuity is preparation. Organizations must first understand their core functions, dependencies, and vulnerabilities through comprehensive business impact analyses. These assessments identify which systems, applications, and services are mission-critical and what the consequences would be if they were interrupted. This information forms the foundation of continuity planning, allowing organizations to prioritize recovery efforts and allocate resources effectively. Resilience is built on this foundation, enhancing systems and processes so they are more resistant to failure and quicker to recover. In digital environments, this might involve deploying redundant systems, implementing failover strategies, and using geographically dispersed data centers to reduce the impact of localized disruptions.

The rise of cloud computing and distributed architectures has transformed how business continuity is approached. While traditional continuity planning often focused on restoring on-premises infrastructure after a disaster, modern strategies leverage cloud capabilities to achieve near-instant recovery and high availability. Services can be replicated across multiple regions, and data can be backed up continuously to ensure minimal loss. However, these benefits also introduce new complexities. Organizations must ensure that their cloud providers meet stringent availability and security requirements, and that failover configurations are tested regularly. The shared responsibility model means that while cloud providers manage the physical infrastructure, the organization remains responsible for data integrity, configuration, and access control.

Cybersecurity threats represent one of the most significant challenges to business continuity. Ransomware attacks, data breaches, and denial-of-service campaigns can cripple operations and cause long-term reputational and financial damage. Therefore, cybersecurity and resilience must be tightly integrated. Proactive defense mechanisms such as threat detection, intrusion prevention, and endpoint protection help reduce the likelihood of an incident. At the same time, resilience measures ensure that if an attack succeeds, the organization can contain its spread, recover systems, and resume operations with minimal impact. Backup strategies, network segmentation, and incident response plans are all critical components of this integrated approach.

Human factors also play a critical role in business continuity and resilience. Employees must be trained to recognize threats, respond to incidents, and execute contingency plans under pressure. Regular drills, simulations, and tabletop exercises help reinforce these skills and ensure that plans are not just theoretical documents but actionable guides. Crisis communication is another vital area. In times of disruption, clear, timely, and accurate communication with employees, customers, partners, and regulators can prevent confusion, maintain trust, and support coordinated responses. A resilient organization empowers its people to act decisively and collaboratively during difficult moments.

Automation and orchestration have become key enablers of resilience. In environments where thousands of services and endpoints are managed, manual response is too slow and error-prone to be effective during a crisis. Automated failover mechanisms, self-healing infrastructure, and playbook-driven incident responses ensure that systems can react to disruptions faster than human operators could. For example, if a service in one region goes offline, traffic can be rerouted automatically to healthy regions, minimizing downtime. Similarly, if a vulnerability is detected, automated scripts can isolate affected systems, apply patches, and restart services without requiring manual intervention. These capabilities reduce recovery time objectives and support continuous operations.

Regulatory compliance and industry standards further underscore the importance of business continuity and resilience. Organizations in sectors such as finance, healthcare, and energy are often subject to strict requirements around availability, data protection, and disaster recovery. Compliance frameworks like ISO 22301, NIST SP 800-34, and GDPR encourage or mandate the implementation of continuity plans, risk assessments, and regular testing. Meeting these requirements is not only a matter of legal obligation but also a competitive advantage. Demonstrating resilience builds confidence among stakeholders and reassures customers that their data and services are protected, even in adverse conditions.

Supply chain resilience is another increasingly important aspect of continuity planning. Modern organizations rely on a complex web of vendors, partners, and third-party services to deliver their products and operate their systems. A disruption at any point in the supply chain can have cascading effects across the business. Therefore, organizations must assess the continuity capabilities of their partners, diversify suppliers where possible, and develop contingency plans for critical dependencies. Contracts and service level agreements should include clear provisions for incident response, availability, and recovery to ensure that third parties contribute to, rather than jeopardize, organizational resilience.

As digital transformation accelerates, resilience must extend beyond technical infrastructure to include data resilience. Data is the lifeblood of modern enterprises, and its availability, integrity, and confidentiality are essential to every business function. Data resilience involves strategies such as replication, versioning, encryption, and real-time backup. These measures ensure that data remains accessible and accurate, even in the face of corruption, deletion, or compromise. Equally important is the ability to recover data quickly. This requires detailed knowledge of where data resides, how it is protected, and how recovery processes are triggered and validated. Effective data resilience minimizes operational disruption and supports compliance with data protection regulations.

Organizational culture plays a crucial role in sustaining business continuity and resilience over time. Leadership must champion these principles, investing in resources, technologies, and training that support long-term preparedness. Risk awareness must permeate all levels of the organization, with employees understanding how their actions impact resilience and what to do when disruptions occur. A culture of continuous improvement ensures that lessons learned from incidents and near-misses are used to refine plans, update technologies, and strengthen defenses. This ongoing commitment to resilience transforms it from a reactive necessity into a strategic asset.

In a world where uncertainty is the only constant, organizations that prioritize business continuity and resilience are better equipped to navigate challenges, protect their assets, and sustain growth. They understand that disruptions will happen and that survival depends not on avoiding them altogether, but on responding with agility, recovering swiftly, and learning from every event. Resilience is not a single system or policy but a mindset, embedded in technology, process, and people, that prepares organizations to thrive in the face of adversity.

Auditing and Regulatory Compliance

Auditing and regulatory compliance have become central components of modern enterprise governance, particularly in an era defined by rapid technological evolution, increasingly sophisticated cyber threats, and growing concerns around data privacy and ethical responsibility. As organizations scale their digital infrastructure, adopt cloud services, and automate more of their operations, the need for transparency, accountability, and adherence to external regulations becomes even more critical. Regulatory frameworks exist to ensure that organizations operate within defined legal and ethical boundaries, protect sensitive information, and maintain the integrity of their systems. Auditing, in turn, serves as a structured mechanism for evaluating whether these obligations are being met consistently and effectively.

At its core, auditing provides an objective, systematic review of an organization's policies, controls, processes, and records. It verifies compliance with internal standards and external regulations, assesses the effectiveness of control mechanisms, and identifies areas for improvement or remediation. In highly regulated industries such as finance, healthcare, and energy, audits are not only expected but mandatory, often carried out by independent third parties to ensure impartiality. Even in less-regulated environments, internal audits are a best practice that allows organizations to detect and address issues before they escalate into violations or breaches.

Regulatory compliance is a broad and multifaceted domain, encompassing international laws, industry-specific standards, and regionally enforced directives. Examples include the General Data Protection Regulation in Europe, which governs the handling of personal data, the Health Insurance Portability and Accountability Act in the United States, which protects healthcare information, and the Sarbanes-Oxley Act, which mandates financial transparency for publicly traded companies. There are also widely adopted standards like ISO/IEC 27001, which provides a framework for information security management systems, and PCI DSS, which governs how payment card data must be protected. Each of these frameworks brings its own set of rules, documentation requirements, technical controls, and enforcement mechanisms.

The challenge for organizations lies in navigating this complex web of requirements while maintaining operational efficiency and agility. Compliance is not simply a matter of ticking boxes or preparing for an annual inspection; it is a continuous, evolving process that must be embedded into daily operations and development workflows. This is especially true in environments that leverage DevOps, agile methodologies, or cloud-native architectures. In such settings, where changes are made rapidly and infrastructure is defined as code, traditional manual compliance checks are no longer sufficient. Automation, integration, and real-time monitoring are necessary to ensure that compliance is maintained without slowing down innovation.

One of the key strategies for aligning auditing and compliance with modern development practices is compliance as code. This approach involves codifying regulatory requirements into automated rules and policies that can be enforced programmatically across infrastructure and applications. Tools that support policy as code allow teams to define guardrails for resource provisioning, access control, data handling, and more. For instance, a policy might prevent the creation of public-facing storage buckets or enforce encryption for data in transit and at rest. These controls are applied automatically during the development or deployment process, ensuring that violations are caught early and do not propagate into production.

Audit trails are another essential component of both auditing and compliance. These are detailed records of actions taken within systems, such as user logins, configuration changes, data access events, and administrative activity. Effective audit trails provide a chronological log of events that can be analyzed to detect anomalies, investigate incidents, or prove compliance during formal audits. In cloud environments, services like AWS CloudTrail, Azure Monitor, and Google Cloud Audit Logs provide native capabilities for tracking activity across the stack. However, organizations must ensure that these logs are centralized, retained according to policy, and protected from tampering. Proper logging enables not only reactive forensics but also proactive risk management.

Risk assessments are closely linked to auditing and are often a prerequisite for achieving compliance. Regulators and standards bodies frequently require organizations to identify, assess, and mitigate potential threats to data and systems. These assessments must be documented and regularly updated to reflect changes in technology, business operations, or the threat landscape. The results of risk assessments inform the design of security controls, the allocation of resources, and the prioritization of remediation efforts. Auditors will examine whether these assessments have been conducted, whether the risks are well understood, and whether adequate steps have been taken to address them.

Documentation is another cornerstone of regulatory compliance. Organizations must be able to produce clear, comprehensive, and accurate documentation that demonstrates how policies are implemented, how controls are monitored, and how incidents are handled. This includes policies on data retention, user access, disaster recovery, and incident response. The documentation must be kept up to date and reviewed periodically. During audits, the absence of documentation or inconsistencies between policy and practice can result in findings that lead to penalties or increased scrutiny. Good documentation also supports institutional memory, ensuring that knowledge is preserved even as personnel or technologies change.

Training and awareness programs are essential to ensure that employees understand their responsibilities related to compliance and the consequences of non-compliance. Regulatory frameworks often require organizations to demonstrate that employees have received appropriate training on security practices, data handling procedures, and ethical conduct. These programs should be tailored to the roles and responsibilities of different users, from technical staff managing infrastructure to customer service representatives handling sensitive client information. Ongoing education reinforces a culture of compliance and reduces the risk of inadvertent violations.

The consequences of non-compliance can be severe. Regulatory violations can result in substantial fines, legal action, loss of business licenses, and damage to an organization's reputation. In some cases, individual executives may be held personally liable for failures in oversight. Beyond the financial and legal penalties, failure to comply can erode customer trust, especially in sectors where data privacy and integrity are paramount. Conversely, strong compliance programs can become a competitive differentiator, signaling to customers, investors, and partners that the organization takes security and governance seriously.

As regulatory landscapes evolve, organizations must remain agile and proactive. New laws are being introduced to address emerging technologies such as artificial intelligence, blockchain, and the Internet of Things. These innovations bring new compliance considerations that go beyond traditional data protection and security requirements. Forward-thinking organizations monitor regulatory developments, participate in industry working groups, and adapt their compliance programs to stay ahead. This adaptability, combined with strong auditing practices and a commitment to transparency, positions them to succeed in a world where regulatory expectations are higher than ever. Auditing and compliance, when treated as integral parts of the organizational fabric, support resilience, foster trust, and enable responsible innovation.

DevSecOps in Financial Services

DevSecOps in financial services represents a critical evolution in the way security is integrated into the software development lifecycle within one of the world's most heavily regulated and high-stakes industries. Financial institutions manage vast amounts of sensitive data, including personal identifiable information, transaction records, and proprietary algorithms. They operate in an environment where trust, uptime, and compliance are paramount. The traditional separation between development, operations, and security teams no longer meets the speed, complexity, or risk demands of modern financial platforms. DevSecOps seeks to address these challenges by embedding security directly into the development pipeline, fostering collaboration, automation, and a shared responsibility model for safeguarding assets.

The financial industry has historically been cautious in adopting new technologies due to the stringent regulatory requirements and the potential impact of failures or breaches. However, the rise of fintech startups, increasing customer expectations for digital services, and the need for agility have pushed even the most conservative banks and financial institutions toward digital transformation. This shift has introduced new complexities and threats, making the integration of security into every phase of development not just beneficial but essential. DevSecOps provides the framework to balance innovation with compliance and security, enabling organizations to release new features quickly while maintaining rigorous control over their systems.

One of the core principles of DevSecOps in financial services is early and continuous security testing. Rather than treating security as a gate that must be passed before deployment, DevSecOps promotes the idea of shifting left—embedding security measures at the very beginning of the development process. Static application security testing (SAST), dynamic application security testing (DAST), and software composition analysis (SCA) tools are integrated directly into the development pipeline. These tools scan code for vulnerabilities, insecure configurations, and third-party library issues as developers write and commit their work. This proactive approach reduces the cost and complexity of remediation by catching issues long before they reach production.

Automation is another key enabler of DevSecOps in financial services. Given the complexity and volume of software systems in this sector, manual security reviews and testing are neither scalable nor reliable. Automated security gates, policy checks, and compliance validations are built into CI/CD pipelines, ensuring that each code change is evaluated consistently against security and regulatory standards. This not only improves efficiency but also helps demonstrate compliance with internal policies and external mandates such as PCI DSS, SOX, or GDPR. Infrastructure as code (IaC) scanning tools analyze cloud templates and configuration scripts to identify potential security missteps before infrastructure is provisioned.

Identity and access management is particularly important in the financial industry, where unauthorized access to systems or data can have devastating consequences. DevSecOps practices emphasize strict access controls, role-based permissions, and the use of secrets management tools to safeguard credentials, tokens, and keys. Integration with centralized identity providers allows for consistent policy enforcement across environments. Additionally, multifactor authentication and just-in-time access models limit exposure by ensuring that access is granted only when and where it is needed. These mechanisms are integrated into the development and deployment lifecycle to reduce the attack surface while maintaining operational flexibility.

Monitoring and observability are crucial for maintaining situational awareness in high-stakes environments. DevSecOps frameworks in financial institutions include robust logging, alerting, and threat detection capabilities that are tightly woven into operational workflows. Logs from applications, services, and infrastructure are centralized and analyzed in real time to detect anomalies, potential breaches, or compliance violations. These systems feed into security information and event management (SIEM) platforms that provide context, correlation, and automated responses. Continuous feedback from monitoring systems informs developers of potential issues and helps refine security controls over time.

Incident response is another area where DevSecOps brings tangible improvements to financial services. In a traditional setup, responding to a breach or failure might involve multiple handoffs, delays, and uncertainty. In a DevSecOps environment, playbooks are automated, teams are cross-functional, and communication is streamlined. Security incidents are treated as high-priority bugs with dedicated resolution pipelines. The ability to rapidly isolate, contain, and remediate threats reduces the window of exposure and minimizes damage. Post-incident reviews contribute to continuous improvement, ensuring that lessons learned lead to better defenses and faster response in the future.

Financial services are also heavily influenced by regulatory bodies and must meet strict compliance requirements. DevSecOps does not eliminate these obligations but rather helps fulfill them more efficiently and transparently. Policy as code allows compliance rules to be codified, version-controlled, and applied automatically across systems. For example, rules about data retention, encryption standards, or access logging can be enforced consistently through automated workflows. Auditors can be provided with clear, traceable evidence of compliance, reducing the burden of manual documentation and increasing confidence in the organization's security posture.

The culture shift required for DevSecOps adoption is significant, especially in industries where silos have long defined workflows. In financial institutions, where development teams, operations teams, and security teams have traditionally functioned independently, moving to a collaborative model requires not only new tools but also a change in mindset. Leadership must champion this transformation, emphasizing the shared responsibility for security and the value of speed with safety. Training, workshops, and internal communities of practice can help bridge knowledge gaps and foster a culture where developers understand security, security teams understand code, and everyone speaks the same language.

Fintech startups have been at the forefront of DevSecOps, using it to build secure, agile systems from the ground up. Their example has shown that speed and security are not mutually exclusive. Established financial institutions are now following suit, often by modernizing legacy systems, adopting cloud platforms, and refactoring applications to support continuous delivery. Hybrid architectures, where cloud-native services interact with traditional core banking systems, require careful orchestration and security integration. DevSecOps provides the necessary framework to manage this complexity without sacrificing control.

As financial services continue to evolve, DevSecOps will play an increasingly central role in enabling secure innovation. The threats facing the industry are dynamic and relentless, but so too are the opportunities for digital transformation. By embedding security into every stage of the development lifecycle, fostering collaboration between teams, and automating compliance and monitoring, financial institutions can build systems that are not only fast and scalable but also resilient and trustworthy. The result is a stronger alignment between business goals, technological capabilities, and the ever-important mandate to protect customer trust and financial integrity.

DevSecOps in Healthcare and Regulated Industries

DevSecOps in healthcare and regulated industries represents a transformative shift in how organizations approach security, compliance, and innovation. These sectors are governed by strict regulatory requirements, face unique security challenges, and operate with a heightened sense of risk due to the sensitive nature of the data they manage. Patient records, proprietary research, pharmaceutical data, and industrial control systems all require the highest levels of protection. At the same time, the demand for agility, efficiency, and technological advancement continues to grow. DevSecOps, which integrates security into every phase of the software development lifecycle, offers a compelling solution to this tension by enabling faster delivery of secure, compliant software in environments where failure is not an option.

In healthcare, for example, digital transformation has accelerated rapidly in recent years, driven by the need for better patient outcomes, more efficient care delivery, and data interoperability. Electronic health records, telemedicine platforms, wearable medical devices, and health information exchanges all generate and process vast amounts of personal health information. This data is not only incredibly valuable to cybercriminals but also subject to regulations such as the Health Insurance Portability and Accountability Act in the United States and the General Data Protection Regulation in Europe. A single security breach can have devastating consequences for patients and providers alike, both in terms of safety and trust. DevSecOps offers a framework in which security is not a barrier to innovation but an enabler of responsible, secure development.

Regulated industries beyond healthcare, such as energy, defense, aviation, and pharmaceuticals, also face a complex blend of innovation and compliance challenges. These sectors often rely on legacy systems that are difficult to modernize yet must remain operational and secure. At the same time, they are under pressure to adopt emerging technologies such as artificial intelligence, machine learning, and the Internet of Things, all of which increase the attack surface and introduce new compliance considerations. DevSecOps supports these transformations by embedding security into development workflows, enforcing policy automatically, and enabling continuous monitoring of systems and data across hybrid environments.

A critical aspect of DevSecOps in regulated environments is compliance automation. Traditional compliance approaches rely heavily on documentation, manual audits, and static policy enforcement. These methods are slow, reactive, and often disconnected from the day-to-day operations of development teams. DevSecOps replaces these siloed processes with policy as code and compliance as code, allowing organizations to codify their regulatory requirements into machine-readable rules that are enforced consistently throughout the development and deployment pipeline. For example, a regulation that requires encryption for data at rest can be translated into a policy that blocks deployment of any infrastructure lacking the appropriate encryption settings. This shift enables compliance to be proactive, integrated, and real-time.

Automation also plays a key role in managing the scale and complexity of regulated systems. Applications in healthcare and other critical sectors are often deployed across multiple environments, including on-premises data centers, cloud platforms, and edge devices. These deployments must be secured, monitored, and validated continuously. DevSecOps promotes the use of automated tools to perform vulnerability scans, analyze dependencies, verify configurations, and validate code quality. These tools are integrated into the CI/CD pipeline to ensure that every change is scrutinized for risk and compliance before it reaches production. Automated testing and validation reduce the likelihood of human error, speed up delivery, and enhance overall system integrity.

Data privacy is another major concern in regulated industries. Personal data, financial data, and intellectual property must be handled with extreme care, especially in environments where data flows between different jurisdictions. DevSecOps supports privacy by design, embedding data protection principles into the development process from the outset. Teams are encouraged to minimize data collection, anonymize sensitive information, and apply strict access controls throughout the software lifecycle. Tools for secrets management, encryption, and access auditing ensure that only authorized users and systems can interact with protected data. These practices help organizations meet regulatory obligations while preserving customer and stakeholder trust.

Incident response and disaster recovery are essential in regulated sectors where availability and reliability are mission-critical. DevSecOps encourages organizations to build automated, repeatable processes for detecting, containing, and recovering from security incidents. When incidents occur, the same CI/CD tools used to deliver software can be leveraged to roll back changes, deploy patches, and reconfigure systems with minimal delay. Post-incident analysis and feedback loops contribute to continuous improvement, enabling organizations to learn from failures and reinforce their defenses. This agility is particularly important in healthcare, where system outages can directly impact patient safety, or in the energy sector, where disruptions can affect national infrastructure.

Collaboration is another pillar of DevSecOps that benefits regulated industries. In traditional models, development, security, compliance, and operations teams work in silos, often leading to friction, delays, and blind spots. DevSecOps breaks down these silos by fostering a culture of shared responsibility and mutual understanding. Cross-functional teams work together to define security requirements, build secure code, and maintain compliant systems. This cultural shift is supported by education, tooling, and leadership commitment. When security and compliance are seen not as obstacles but as integral parts of the development process, organizations can move faster and with greater confidence.

Visibility and auditability are crucial for satisfying regulators and maintaining internal governance. DevSecOps emphasizes the creation of detailed logs, traceable artifacts, and transparent workflows that can be reviewed and audited at any time. Every code change, infrastructure modification, and deployment event is logged, enabling organizations to demonstrate compliance and investigate issues with precision. Dashboards and reporting tools provide real-time insights into system health, risk posture, and regulatory adherence. This transparency supports internal decision-making, regulatory reporting, and third-party assessments, making it easier to pass audits and avoid penalties.

Training and awareness are vital to sustaining DevSecOps in regulated industries. Security and compliance are not the sole responsibility of a few experts; they require a collective commitment across the organization. Developers must be trained in secure coding practices and data protection principles. Operations teams need to understand how to monitor and maintain compliant environments. Security professionals must stay informed about emerging threats and evolving regulations. Continuous education, role-specific training, and practical simulations help build a workforce that is equipped to uphold security and compliance at all levels.

DevSecOps is not a one-size-fits-all solution but a flexible framework that can be tailored to the specific needs of different industries and regulatory contexts. In healthcare and regulated sectors, it provides a path forward—one that supports innovation without compromising security, speeds up delivery without losing control, and builds trust without sacrificing agility. By embedding security and compliance into the fabric of development, DevSecOps empowers organizations to meet the highest standards of safety, reliability, and accountability in a rapidly changing world.

Building a DevSecOps Team

Building a DevSecOps team is a strategic undertaking that goes far beyond hiring a few security professionals and assigning them to a software development project. It requires rethinking how organizations structure their teams, how they define roles and responsibilities, and how they cultivate a culture of collaboration, ownership, and continuous improvement. DevSecOps is fundamentally about integrating security into every phase óf the development lifecycle, from planning and coding to deployment and operations. To accomplish this, organizations must form cross-functional teams that bring together developers, operations engineers, and security professionals with a shared mission: to deliver secure, reliable, and high-quality software at speed.

One of the first steps in building a successful DevSecOps team is aligning leadership around the vision and goals of DevSecOps.

Without executive support, the initiative is unlikely to gain traction. Leadership must recognize that security is not a final checkpoint or a separate department, but a core quality attribute of software that must be built in from the beginning. This understanding sets the tone for the organization and ensures that the necessary resources—both human and technological—are allocated to support the transformation. It also sends a clear message that security is a shared responsibility and not just the concern of a single team.

Recruiting the right talent is a crucial element in forming a DevSecOps team. Traditional roles such as developers, system administrators, and security analysts are still essential, but the boundaries between these roles begin to blur in a DevSecOps environment. Developers are expected to have a foundational understanding of security principles. Security experts must be comfortable working with code, automation tools, and cloud infrastructure. Operations engineers need to understand how to enforce security policies through configuration management and monitoring systems. The most successful DevSecOps teams are composed of individuals who are not only experts in their domains but also possess a willingness to learn, adapt, and collaborate across disciplines.

In addition to hiring new talent, organizations must invest in upskilling existing team members. Many companies already have capable professionals who can transition into DevSecOps roles with the right training and support. Offering learning opportunities, such as workshops, certifications, and hands-on labs, helps bridge skill gaps and fosters a culture of continuous improvement. Pair programming, code reviews, and collaborative design sessions are also effective ways to spread security knowledge and build trust among team members. Encouraging cross-training between developers, security, and operations roles helps ensure that the team can function cohesively and respond quickly to challenges.

The structure of a DevSecOps team can vary depending on the size and needs of the organization, but some core principles remain constant. The team should be cross-functional, with members embedded throughout the development lifecycle. Rather than creating a separate DevSecOps unit that operates in isolation, organizations should distribute security expertise within development squads or product teams. This approach allows security practices to scale with the organization and ensures that every team has the tools and knowledge needed to make secure decisions. A centralized security group may still exist to provide guidance, maintain standards, and develop reusable tools, but the implementation and enforcement of security controls happen within each team.

Communication is the glue that holds a DevSecOps team together. Transparent, frequent, and open communication helps align priorities, resolve conflicts, and ensure that everyone is working toward common goals. Daily stand-ups, retrospectives, and planning meetings provide opportunities to surface security concerns early and integrate them into the workflow. Tools that support real-time collaboration—such as shared repositories, issue trackers, and chat platforms—enable teams to document decisions, share knowledge, and stay informed. Security must not be seen as a blocker or gatekeeper but as a partner that helps the team move faster and with greater confidence.

Automation is a defining characteristic of DevSecOps, and the team must be equipped to build and maintain automated security pipelines. This includes integrating tools for static and dynamic code analysis, dependency scanning, secret detection, configuration validation, and vulnerability management into the CI/CD process. The team should also define and enforce policies using infrastructure as code and policy as code tools, ensuring that environments are provisioned securely and consistently. Automation reduces the burden on individual team members, minimizes human error, and enables rapid feedback loops that support agile development practices.

Metrics and feedback are essential for guiding and evaluating the performance of a DevSecOps team. The team should define key performance indicators that reflect both security and development goals. These might include the number of vulnerabilities detected and remediated, the time to patch critical issues, the frequency of secure code releases, or the reduction in policy violations over time. Regularly reviewing these metrics helps the team identify areas for improvement, celebrate successes, and demonstrate the value of DevSecOps to stakeholders. Feedback loops also support adaptive planning and ensure that the team remains responsive to changing requirements and threats.

Fostering a culture of psychological safety is vital for encouraging innovation and continuous learning within a DevSecOps team. Team members must feel comfortable raising concerns, admitting mistakes, and proposing new ideas without fear of blame or punishment. Leaders should model humility, curiosity, and accountability, creating an environment where experimentation is encouraged and failures are seen as learning opportunities. Blameless postmortems, open knowledge sharing, and recognition of individual contributions all contribute to a healthy team culture that supports long-term success.

Security champions can play a powerful role in scaling DevSecOps practices across an organization. These are individuals within development or operations teams who take on additional responsibilities for promoting security awareness, advocating best practices, and serving as liaisons with the central security team. By empowering security champions with training, resources, and support, organizations can extend the reach of their DevSecOps initiatives and ensure that security considerations are present in every conversation, design decision, and line of code.

As organizations evolve, so too must their DevSecOps teams. New technologies, compliance requirements, and threat landscapes will demand new skills, tools, and approaches. The most resilient teams are those that embrace change, remain curious, and commit to lifelong learning. Building a DevSecOps team is not a one-time project but an ongoing journey—one that requires patience, investment, and a shared vision of what secure, agile, and high-performing software development can truly look like. By bringing together the right people, cultivating a collaborative culture, and embedding security into every part of the process, organizations can create teams that not only deliver value but also protect it at every turn.

Training and Upskilling for DevSecOps

Training and upskilling for DevSecOps is a vital investment for organizations striving to integrate security seamlessly into their development and operations pipelines. As technology rapidly evolves, the traditional silos between development, operations, and security become counterproductive. DevSecOps calls for a collaborative, agile, and security-first mindset that requires all team members to possess a foundational understanding of security principles and the ability to apply them in real time. For this transformation to succeed, organizations must foster a learning culture, provide structured educational paths, and ensure continuous professional growth across all roles involved in software delivery.

One of the foundational challenges in adopting DevSecOps is the skill gap that exists between development, security, and operations professionals. Developers are often not trained in secure coding practices or common vulnerabilities. Security experts may lack hands-on experience with modern automation tools or cloud-native architectures. Operations teams might be unfamiliar with the nuances of application-layer security or secure provisioning in dynamic environments. Bridging these gaps requires a comprehensive and ongoing training strategy that goes beyond occasional workshops or certifications. It demands an organizational shift toward continuous learning and cross-disciplinary collaboration.

A successful DevSecOps training program begins with a clear understanding of the roles and responsibilities within a DevSecOps environment. While specialization remains important, the boundaries between roles become more fluid. Developers are expected to understand how their code affects system security and stability. Security professionals must be able to contribute to automation efforts, write scripts, and engage in code reviews. Operations teams must be comfortable implementing infrastructure as code and integrating security policies into provisioning workflows. To support this, training should be personalized and role-specific, ensuring that each team member receives the knowledge and hands-on experience relevant to their day-to-day responsibilities.

Hands-on learning is essential for meaningful skill development in DevSecOps. Theory alone cannot prepare individuals to secure complex, fast-moving environments. Practical exercises, simulations, and lab environments allow learners to engage with real tools and scenarios. These experiences can include everything from securing a containerized application in Kubernetes, to scanning infrastructure as code templates for misconfigurations, to writing custom policies for compliance as code tools. Immersive learning environments that replicate production conditions enable learners to develop muscle memory, build confidence, and respond effectively to real-world challenges.

Gamification and interactive learning platforms can also enhance the upskilling experience. Capture the flag competitions, red vs. blue team exercises, and scenario-based challenges introduce elements of competition and fun, making security training more engaging and memorable. These activities promote problem-solving, teamwork, and critical thinking under pressure—all key attributes in a DevSecOps culture. Organizations that incorporate these elements into their training programs often see greater participation, retention, and enthusiasm from their teams.

Another important component of upskilling for DevSecOps is integrating training into the existing workflows of development and operations. Instead of pulling teams away from their work for long, infrequent training sessions, learning opportunities should be embedded into daily routines. Contextual learning tools, such as IDE plugins that flag insecure code or CI/CD pipeline feedback that highlights policy violations, help developers learn while they work. Microlearning platforms that deliver short, focused lessons at the point of need make it easier for team members to absorb and apply new knowledge without disrupting productivity.

Mentorship and peer learning are powerful tools for cultivating DevSecOps skills across an organization. Senior engineers, security champions, and experienced DevOps practitioners can guide newer team members, offer practical advice, and model best practices. Pair programming, peer code reviews, and collaborative threat modeling sessions create opportunities for knowledge transfer and foster a sense of shared responsibility for security. Encouraging open dialogue and a willingness to ask questions helps break down barriers between disciplines and accelerates the spread of security awareness across teams.

To sustain momentum and ensure long-term success, organizations should support formal certifications and ongoing professional development. Certifications such as Certified DevSecOps Professional,

Offensive Security Certified Professional, or cloud-specific security credentials from AWS, Azure, and Google Cloud provide recognition and structure to individual learning journeys. Reimbursing certification costs, allocating time for study, and celebrating achievements all signal the organization's commitment to growth and learning. In industries where compliance and regulation are key concerns, these certifications also demonstrate to stakeholders that staff possess the requisite skills to operate securely and responsibly.

Leadership plays a critical role in driving DevSecOps training initiatives. Executives and managers must champion the value of upskilling and allocate resources to support it. This includes not only funding but also time, tools, and internal platforms for knowledge sharing. Training should be tied to performance metrics, career development plans, and organizational goals. When employees see that their learning is valued, supported, and aligned with business objectives, they are more likely to engage with training programs and take ownership of their development.

Measuring the impact of DevSecOps training requires both qualitative and quantitative metrics. Organizations can track the number of team members completing training, earning certifications, or participating in security initiatives. They can also monitor improvements in code quality, reduction in vulnerabilities, faster incident response times, and better audit outcomes. Feedback surveys and retrospective meetings can provide insight into what's working and what needs improvement. These metrics help refine training programs and ensure they continue to meet the evolving needs of the organization.

Building a successful DevSecOps culture depends not only on tools and processes but on people who understand and embrace the principles of secure, collaborative development. Training and upskilling are the catalysts for this transformation. By investing in continuous learning, fostering cross-functional understanding, and creating opportunities for hands-on experience, organizations empower their teams to innovate securely and respond confidently to emerging threats. The journey to DevSecOps maturity is ongoing, but with a strong foundation of education and support, teams can rise to meet the challenges of modern software development and build systems that are not only fast and scalable but resilient and secure.

DevSecOps Maturity Models

DevSecOps maturity models serve as a structured framework for organizations to assess, guide, and improve their security integration within the software development lifecycle. As organizations adopt DevSecOps practices, they often find themselves progressing through different levels of maturity, each representing a deeper alignment of development, security, and operations. These models are not rigid checklists but flexible roadmaps that help teams understand where they stand, where they aim to go, and what steps are necessary to advance. A well-implemented maturity model not only measures technical capabilities but also reflects cultural readiness, collaboration, process consistency, and the extent of automation across the pipeline.

In the early stages of DevSecOps maturity, security is often reactive and isolated. Organizations at this level might rely on manual security checks performed late in the development process, typically just before deployment. These checks are usually handled by a separate security team, creating bottlenecks, delays, and friction between teams. There may be limited awareness among developers about secure coding practices, and security incidents are typically addressed after they occur rather than prevented in advance. While some security tools might be in use, they are rarely integrated into the CI/CD pipeline, and their findings may not be consistently actioned. This stage reflects a traditional, siloed approach where security is treated more as a compliance necessity than a shared responsibility.

As organizations begin to move toward a more integrated model, they often reach a transitional phase where security is introduced earlier in the development lifecycle, albeit in a somewhat ad hoc manner. In this intermediate maturity level, security teams start working more closely with developers and operations teams. Static analysis tools, dependency checks, and container scans may be introduced into development workflows, and there is a growing emphasis on education and awareness. Developers begin to take ownership of security within their code, and operations teams become more involved in monitoring for security-related issues in production environments. However, automation may still be limited, and policies may not be consistently enforced across environments. This phase represents a growing recognition of the value of DevSecOps but with uneven implementation.

Organizations that progress further achieve a more structured and automated approach. Security becomes a continuous, integrated process that spans planning, development, testing, deployment, and monitoring. Automation is a hallmark of this level of maturity. Security controls are embedded directly into the CI/CD pipeline, including automated scans, policy enforcement, and infrastructure validation. Compliance requirements are codified into machine-readable policies that can be applied and audited in real time. Developers, security professionals, and operations teams collaborate as part of a unified workflow, sharing tools, metrics, and feedback loops. Security incidents are not only resolved efficiently but also used as learning opportunities to improve defenses across the system. The organization at this stage has embraced security as a core quality attribute, built into every component of the software delivery process.

At the highest level of DevSecOps maturity, security becomes not just embedded but adaptive. The organization operates with a culture of continuous improvement, where security practices evolve in response to changing threats, new technologies, and shifting business needs. Threat modeling is performed proactively during the design phase, and risk assessments are conducted dynamically based on real-time telemetry. Advanced analytics, artificial intelligence, and machine learning may be used to detect anomalies and predict security risks before they manifest. Security testing and validation are fully automated, continuous, and scalable across environments. Feedback from incidents, red team exercises, and threat intelligence feeds directly into development pipelines, enabling systems to self-correct and improve. Cross-functional teams operate with a shared language and mission, and the organization can demonstrate measurable, repeatable, and auditable security performance aligned with its business goals.

Cultural transformation is a critical dimension of DevSecOps maturity. Without a cultural foundation that supports collaboration, accountability, and trust, even the most advanced tools and processes will fall short. Maturity models help organizations assess cultural indicators, such as how openly teams communicate, how frequently security is discussed in planning meetings, and how well individuals understand their role in maintaining security. These softer metrics are just as important as technical indicators because they influence how effectively DevSecOps principles are internalized and practiced on a daily basis. As organizations mature, they shift from a blame-oriented culture to one that encourages experimentation, learning from mistakes, and continuous feedback.

Governance and compliance maturity also evolves with DevSecOps. In early stages, compliance may be achieved through manual audits and reactive documentation. As maturity increases, organizations begin to automate compliance evidence collection, enforce policies as code, and integrate governance into the development workflow. This transition makes it easier to meet regulatory obligations while reducing overhead and error. In highly mature organizations, compliance becomes continuous and transparent. Auditors can access real-time evidence, and development teams can deploy code with confidence, knowing that it adheres to both internal standards and external regulations.

Metrics play a crucial role in understanding and advancing DevSecOps maturity. Organizations must identify and track key performance indicators that reflect both security effectiveness and development agility. Metrics might include the time it takes to resolve vulnerabilities, the number of automated security checks per release, the percentage of coverage by security testing tools, or the frequency of policy violations. These metrics should be visible, actionable, and tied to improvement goals. Maturity models guide organizations in defining which metrics are relevant at each stage and how to interpret them in the context of strategic objectives.

Every organization's DevSecOps journey is unique. Maturity models are not about achieving perfection but about making informed decisions and setting realistic goals based on current capabilities and future needs. They provide a structured language for discussing progress, identifying gaps, and allocating resources. Whether an organization is just beginning to explore DevSecOps or already operates at a high level of maturity, the model serves as a compass, pointing the way toward more secure, resilient, and efficient software delivery. By continuously assessing maturity and committing to growth, organizations position themselves to thrive in an increasingly complex and threat-laden digital landscape.

Future Trends in DevSecOps

Future trends in DevSecOps are shaped by the growing complexity of software systems, the acceleration of digital transformation, and the increasingly sophisticated nature of cybersecurity threats. As organizations continue to move toward agile and cloud-native architectures, the need to embed security deeper into the software development lifecycle becomes even more urgent. DevSecOps, which integrates security into development and operations workflows, is evolving rapidly in response to these pressures. In the coming years, it is expected to become more intelligent, more automated, and more adaptive, driven by innovations in artificial intelligence, machine learning, infrastructure automation, and regulatory landscapes.

One of the most significant trends in the future of DevSecOps is the deeper integration of artificial intelligence and machine learning into security processes. Traditional rule-based security tools are limited in their ability to detect novel threats or adapt to changing environments. Machine learning models can analyze vast volumes of telemetry data, detect patterns, and identify anomalies far more efficiently than human analysts. In the context of DevSecOps, this means AI-powered tools will increasingly handle threat detection, vulnerability prioritization, and even automated remediation. These systems will not only respond to threats in real time but also learn from past incidents to improve accuracy and reduce false positives, allowing teams to focus on high-priority risks.

Another emerging trend is the increasing adoption of security-as-code. This concept extends the infrastructure-as-code philosophy by embedding security policies directly into the development and deployment pipelines. In the future, organizations will rely more heavily on policy-as-code frameworks that define and enforce rules about encryption, access control, resource provisioning, and compliance. These policies will be version-controlled, tested, and automatically applied, ensuring consistency across environments. The evolution of these practices will lead to more sophisticated, context-aware policies that adapt based on the environment, the risk level of a change, or even the sensitivity of the data involved.

The rise of cloud-native technologies continues to influence DevSecOps practices. Microservices, containers, and serverless architectures introduce new security challenges, including increased surface area, dynamic workloads, and ephemeral resources. In response, DevSecOps tooling will become more lightweight, scalable, and integrated with orchestration platforms like Kubernetes. Future tools will be built to support distributed, hybrid, and multi-cloud environments from the ground up, enabling seamless visibility and control regardless of where workloads are running. Runtime protection, real-time scanning, and behavioral analytics will be embedded into service meshes and container runtimes, providing defense mechanisms that are both proactive and responsive.

As infrastructure and applications become more dynamic, observability will become even more critical. The future of DevSecOps includes more advanced observability tools that combine telemetry from logs, metrics, traces, and user behavior to provide a comprehensive security picture. These tools will not only alert teams to suspicious activity but also offer insights into the root cause and potential impact of an incident. Coupled with AI and automation, observability will enable near-instantaneous responses to threats, automated incident playbooks, and predictive risk scoring. Teams will shift from reactive security monitoring to proactive risk management, using insights to prevent issues before they manifest.

The increasing complexity of regulatory requirements around data privacy and cybersecurity will also shape the future of DevSecOps. As governments and industry bodies introduce stricter laws, compliance will need to be integrated directly into development and deployment processes. Continuous compliance will replace periodic audits, enabled by automated tools that validate systems against regulatory controls in real time. Developers will receive immediate feedback when a change introduces a compliance violation, and auditors will have access to immutable logs and real-time evidence of adherence to standards. This transformation will make it easier for organizations to scale securely while demonstrating accountability and transparency.

Zero trust architecture is gaining momentum as a response to the changing threat landscape, and it will become a key component of DevSecOps. The principle of never trusting and always verifying applies across every layer of the system, from user identities and network access to service-to-service communication. DevSecOps teams will increasingly adopt tools and practices that enforce zero trust policies, such as identity-based access controls, encryption in transit and at rest, and continuous authentication. These measures will be automated and codified, reducing the complexity of maintaining strict security postures in highly distributed environments.

Training and education will evolve alongside the technology. As DevSecOps becomes more ingrained in organizational culture, teams will need ongoing, role-specific training to stay current with tools, threats, and best practices. Future training programs will include immersive simulations, gamified learning, and AI-driven personal learning paths tailored to individual skill gaps. Organizations will increasingly invest in internal security champions programs, cross-training initiatives, and knowledge-sharing communities to ensure that security literacy permeates every part of the software delivery pipeline.

Collaboration between teams will also deepen, facilitated by more integrated platforms that bring together development, security, operations, and compliance functions. Toolchains will become more unified, offering end-to-end visibility, shared dashboards, and centralized policy management. This convergence will reduce friction between teams and foster a more cohesive approach to risk management. As silos break down, organizations will be better equipped to respond quickly to incidents, adapt to change, and innovate securely.

The future of DevSecOps will also be shaped by the increasing role of automation in governance and risk management. Automated governance will go beyond policy enforcement to include decision-making support for risk acceptance, exception handling, and resource allocation. Systems will be capable of evaluating the security posture of proposed changes, estimating their risk impact, and approving or rejecting them based on predefined criteria. This level of automation will reduce decision fatigue, eliminate human bottlenecks, and ensure that security decisions are made consistently and transparently.

DevSecOps will continue to expand into new domains, including edge computing, the Internet of Things, and embedded systems. As organizations deploy software to more diverse and decentralized environments, security practices will need to extend beyond traditional data centers and cloud environments. Lightweight, distributed security agents, real-time telemetry, and remote update capabilities will become essential components of DevSecOps strategies for these emerging technologies. Security will need to be built into devices from the start, monitored continuously, and updated seamlessly to address evolving threats.

In the years ahead, DevSecOps will no longer be seen as an optional enhancement or a niche methodology. It will be a baseline expectation for software development, embedded into organizational DNA alongside agility, quality, and user experience. As tools become more intelligent, processes more automated, and teams more integrated, DevSecOps will redefine how organizations build and maintain trust in the digital world. This future demands not just better technology, but a relentless commitment to collaboration, adaptability, and continuous improvement across every layer of the software delivery ecosystem.

Final Thoughts and Call to Action

The journey toward fully adopting DevSecOps is both a technical evolution and a cultural transformation. Organizations today are operating in a world of constant change, increasing complexity, and unprecedented risk. With the explosive growth of cloud-native applications, global connectivity, and relentless cyber threats, the imperative to build secure, resilient systems from the ground up has never been greater. DevSecOps is not just a methodology or a toolset— it is a mindset that places security at the heart of innovation, making it an inherent part of how software is conceived, developed, delivered, and maintained.

The integration of security into development and operations workflows is not an overnight transition. It requires careful planning, persistent effort, and a commitment to collaboration across all parts of the organization. Leaders must prioritize security as a business enabler rather than a cost center or obstacle. They must recognize that in a digital economy, trust is currency, and maintaining that trust depends on the integrity of the systems, processes, and teams behind the technology. By embedding security into every layer of the development lifecycle, organizations can move faster without sacrificing control, deliver value while reducing risk, and respond to change with confidence rather than fear.

A successful DevSecOps transformation begins with awareness. Teams must understand not only the technical challenges they face but also the cultural and organizational dynamics that influence how work gets done. It is not enough to purchase security tools or hire more security professionals. The real challenge lies in breaking down silos, fostering mutual respect between teams, and creating an environment where everyone feels responsible for security. When developers, operations engineers, and security professionals work together toward shared goals, they can build systems that are both innovative and secure by design.

Education plays a crucial role in sustaining this shift. Upskilling team members, providing hands-on training, and promoting ongoing learning are all essential components of a DevSecOps culture. Organizations that invest in their people—offering not just instruction but real opportunities for growth and experimentation—will be better equipped to handle the evolving threat landscape. Training should be practical, continuous, and relevant to the technologies in use. Teams should be encouraged to participate in knowledge sharing, cross-functional exercises, and community-driven initiatives that help reinforce a culture of security excellence.

The technology stack itself must also evolve to support DevSecOps principles. Automation is no longer optional. Security controls must be embedded into continuous integration and continuous delivery pipelines. Code must be tested for vulnerabilities as it is written. Infrastructure must be validated before it is deployed. Monitoring and logging must provide real-time visibility into system behavior and potential threats. These capabilities enable organizations to detect, respond to, and recover from incidents quickly—minimizing impact and maintaining business continuity. They also support regulatory compliance by ensuring that policies are enforced consistently and that evidence is available when needed.

Organizations must also embrace the idea of continuous improvement. DevSecOps is not a destination but a journey—one that evolves with each project, release, and incident. Feedback loops are essential, not only for refining code and infrastructure but for refining processes, team dynamics, and strategic priorities. Retrospectives, post-incident reviews, and security audits should be viewed as opportunities for growth rather than exercises in blame. By learning from mistakes and iterating on what works, teams become more agile, resilient, and capable over time.

The future of secure software development will be shaped by those who are willing to challenge outdated assumptions and lead with intention. That means questioning the traditional role of security as a gatekeeper and instead positioning it as a collaborative partner. It means shifting from reactive models of security to proactive, preventative strategies that are integrated from the first line of code. It means creating teams that value diversity of thought, embrace complexity, and are empowered to make decisions that balance risk and innovation.

For those just beginning their DevSecOps journey, the path may seem daunting. The scope of change—technical, organizational, cultural—can appear overwhelming. But progress does not require perfection. Every small step toward integrating security more deeply into the development process contributes to a stronger foundation. Start by identifying quick wins, such as integrating a security scanner into your build process or hosting a threat modeling session with your development team. Celebrate those wins and use them to build momentum. Over time, these incremental improvements compound, leading to more secure systems, more capable teams, and more resilient organizations.

For organizations already practicing DevSecOps, the next challenge is to scale these efforts and sustain the culture of security. This may involve formalizing security policies as code, automating governance controls, or investing in advanced detection and response capabilities. It may involve expanding training programs, mentoring security champions, or aligning DevSecOps practices with broader risk management frameworks. Whatever the specific initiatives, the goal is to ensure that security remains a dynamic, evolving part of the organization's DNA—one that adapts to new threats, new technologies, and new business imperatives.

At the global level, DevSecOps is contributing to a larger shift in how society approaches digital trust. As more systems become interconnected, and as more data is exchanged across borders and platforms, the importance of building secure, transparent, and accountable systems grows. Organizations that embrace DevSecOps not only protect their own assets and reputations—they also contribute to a more secure and trustworthy digital ecosystem. They become leaders in a movement that values safety, privacy, and integrity alongside speed, efficiency, and innovation.

Now is the time for action. The threats facing modern organizations are real, persistent, and constantly evolving. The pace of innovation shows no signs of slowing, and the demand for digital services continues to grow. Waiting for a perfect moment to start integrating security into your development lifecycle is not a viable strategy. The opportunity to lead, to innovate securely, and to build systems that users can trust is available to those willing to commit to the principles and practices of DevSecOps. The responsibility lies with each team, each leader, and each organization to take the next step—no matter how small—and move forward with clarity, courage, and purpose.

www.ingramcontent.com/pod-product-compliance
Lightning Source LLC
LaVergne TN
LVHW051236050326
832903LV00028B/2428